TEXT ○
JOHN BARBER

DESIGN AND PHOTOGRAPHY ○
DAVID A. MAGEE

CONTENTS

INTRODUCTION

1 THE SKELETON: THE GEOLOGY AND GEOMORPHOLOGY of THE ISLANDS

2 THE THAW: AFTER THE ICE AGE

3 HIGH SUMMER: CLIMATIC IMPROVEMENT AND THE ARRIVAL of THE FIRST FARMERS

4 THE RAINY SEASON: CLIMATIC DETERIORATION AND THE DEVELOPMENT of THE BRONZE AGE

5 THE PEAT: CELTIC WARRIORS IN A DROWNING LANDSCAPE

6 LIGHT AND DARK: THE ARRIVAL of CHRISTIANITY AND THE COMING of THE VIKINGS

7 ECHOES of THE LORDSHIP of THE ISLES: ASPECTS of POST-MEDIEVAL SETTLEMENTS DEDUCED FROM SEVENTEENTH CENTURY RECORDS

8 IN LIVING MEMORY

9 GAZETTEER of ARCHAEOLOGICAL SITES

FURTHER READING

LoCATioN

Lewis

Great Bernera

Scarp

Taransay

Scalpay

North Uist

Pabbay

Berneray

Benbecula

Ronay

Harris

South Uist

Barra

Eriskay

Sandray

Berneray

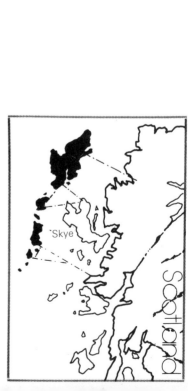

Skye

Scotland

iNTRO

This book has been specifically designed to fall between at least two stools. It is not a guidebook to the Western Isles, nor is it an academic account of their prehistory and early history, although it tries to be something of both. In general it is an attempt at a natural history of the Isles with particular emphasis on man's part in the creation of the several elements which make up the Hebridean landscape. We have tried to concentrate on those sites which are visible to the modern traveller and on those topics which would have occupied the mind of that great Victorian creation, the informed layman. In doing this we have skated over ice so thin that it is, in places, non-existent and have treated as simple statements of fact matters over which vast quantities of academic anguish and ink, if not blood, have been shed. Our only excuse for doing this lies in our desire to lay siege to the imagination of the reader in the hope that awakened interest may drive him on to further enquiry.

We are grateful to the National Museum of Antiquities of Scotland for permission to reproduce Figs. (1−8). In particular we gratefully acknowledge the assistance of Mr Trevor Cowie of the National Museum for help and advice in the selection of these. To Miss D. Lehane for her support and encouragement throughout, and for typing the text, but most of all for her unfailing cheerfulness goes our deepest gratitude.

THE SKELETON

THE GEOLOGY AND GEOMORPHOLOGY of THE ISLANDS

Lying off the western edge of the European continent, the Western Isles have preserved many features and ways of life which time and progress have destroyed, or changed beyond recognition in areas closer to the greater centres of power. The very rock which makes up the skeleton of the 208km (130 mile) island chain is an example of just such archaic survival. Formed in the geologically remote past, the Lewisian Gneiss (pronounced 'nice') of which all the islands are formed is amongst the oldest rocks on earth, being as much as four thousand million years old, in part. The truly incredible length of this timescale may be more readily appreciated when we remember that life itself is only six hundred million years old and man has only begun to evolve as an identifiable entity a mere one and a half to two million years ago. The parent rocks from which the gneiss derives have been considerably altered, or metamorphosed, since their formation, mainly as a result of the very high pressure and temperatures associated with mountain formation. The first of these about which we are aware is called the Scourian Orogeny (orogeny means 'mountain forming period') and took place two thousand five hundred million years ago. This was followed by the Laxfordian Orogeny, just under a billion years later, at about one thousand six hundred million years ago. The extent of metamorphosis is such that it is often very difficult to determine the nature of the original parent rocks, but two broad categories of Lewisian Gneiss can be identified.

▓▓▓	Stornoway beds
■	Granitic
▒▒	'Grey' Gneiss
——	Thrust
– · –	Fault

(Geological map of the Western Isles.)

Timescale — From 4 km to present.

Km   3   2   1   900

Lewisian Gneiss Formed   Scourian Orogeny   Laxfordian Orogeny

4

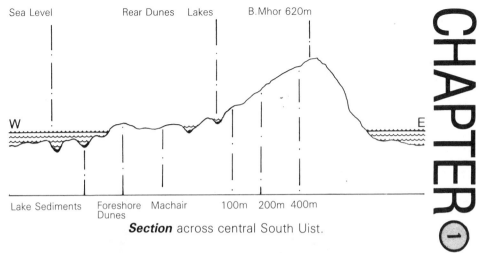

Section across central South Uist.

W .... E

Sea Level   Rear Dunes   Lakes   B.Mhor 620m

Lake Sediments   Foreshore   Machair   100m   200m   400m
Dunes

Typical Hebridean **skyline** viewed from the Callers Way (North Uist)

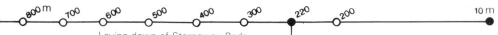

800 m   700   600   500   400   300   220   200   10 m

Laying down of Stornoway Beds

Tertiary Period

Widespread erosion and development of Drainage

The first of these, the Paragneisses, are derived from sedimentary rocks, i.e. rocks like sandstone and limestone which were originally formed under water. The Orthogneisses are derived from igneous rocks like lavas and basalts which originated beneath the earth's crust. Most of the Western Isles are formed of the Orthogneisses, although Paragneisses are dominant in the south-west of Harris. The typical banded gneiss is visible everywhere in the alternating stripes of white and grey or black or more rarely pink in which individual crystals, or platelets, of mica can be seen.

Looking now at the low rounded profiles of the island's hills, it is hard to imagine that once they formed mountains as high as the modern Himalaya. The highest peak in the islands, the Clisham, in Harris is a mere 799m (2,622ft) high, and although low by the general standard of mountains in the Highlands, it towers over the islands, most of whose land surfaces lie below 50m (c.150ft) over sea level. The sea, rain, wind, and frost, the small but persistent forces of erosion, operating over thousands of millions of years, have levelled the great mountains and ground down to the surface of the gneiss. The Tertiary period seems to have been one of large scale and accelerated erosion, and it has been calculated that in Rhum and Skye some 1000m of rock was removed during this period, while on Arran a staggering 2500m (almost two miles thickness) of rock was removed by erosion during the Tertiary period. It was during the Tertiary period that the 'islands' skeleton of Lewisian Gneiss was sculpted to the low planar profile it now posesses. This, originally relatively level surface was subsequently scoured by the Quaternary ice sheets. These, exploiting lines of weakness in the gneiss, have hollowed out strings of shallow depressions many of which were then lined with boulder clay from the ice, ensuring their waterlogging in the post-glacial period. Thus was produced by the combined effects of Tertiary weathering, the characteristic Lewisian and Quaternary ice-sculpting landscape of 'knock and lochan' (or hill-and-little-lake). There are many areas in the islands, particularly in the north-east of North Uist, where water-filled, ice-scoured hollows alternate with low hills in a landscape which often seems more composed of water than land. It was during the Quaternary Ice Age that the mountainous spine of the Western Isles was breached and the original Long Island divided into a number of large islands accompanied by a myriad of small islands.

Exposed quarry face of Gneiss

Quaternary Period

3   2   1·5   1   1m

ICE AGE BEGINS

complicated, and for a long time the relative sea and land levels seesawed up and down, creating a series of raised beaches of which the 50ft and 100ft are the best known (though even these are not simple entities since they commonly occur at heights other than those implied by their titles). These raised beaches are important for most of Scotland in that the earliest humans to settle here occupied the raised beach platforms. However, the picture in the Western Isles is rather different. The islands lay close to the margin of the ice sheets; there are for example no glacial erratics on the islands in the St. Kilda group which lie 50km to the west of the Western Isles, which implies that the ice sheet did not extend that far. Furthermore the land area of the islands is not great, so that the weight of the ice sheets in the region must have been largely supported by the sea. Thus the earth's crust was not, in fact, greatly depressed in the area of the islands and the islands, in turn, have not risen from the post-glacial sea. The raised beaches which form such a distinct and characteristic feature of the west coast of the mainland are, in consequence, absent from the islands. Recent evidence suggests that the sea is steadily gaining of the land in the Western Isles, and estimates of 1m rise in sea level per thousand years have been suggested, particularly for the area of the Uists and Benbecula. Fisherman's nets occasionally bring up lumps of peat or pieces of wood from peat beds which are now up to 5m below mean sea level. These peat beds originally formed in ice-sculpted hollows in the gneiss, and radiocarbon dating indicates that they were being formed about six thousand years ago. Comparable intertidal peat beds can be seen on the west coast of the islands at times of especially low tides. Good examples are visible on the south-west side of Hogharry Bay and nearby at Balelone, both in North Uist.

During the Pleistocene the weight of the great ice sheet resting on mainland Scotland depressed the surface of the earth. When the ice sheets melted, the level of the sea rose rapidly and beaches were formed along the margin of these. Freed of the weight of the ice, the land slowly rose again to approximately its original level, and the early post-glacial beaches can now be found up to 30m (100ft) above current sea level. In practice this process was rather

1m   900000   800000   700000   600000

These submerged peat beds are not to be confused with the eroding peat beds which are a common sight on the west coasts of Benbecula and South Uist. There the rising sea has begun to cut into peat deposits — in some cases quite deep deposits — which are formed on dry land. Visitors passing to Benbecula over the causeway from South Uist and taking the minor coast road thence to Ballivanich will see some splendid examples of peat 'cliffs' in excess of six foot high undergoing erosion by the rising sea. Further north, near the Inn at Carinish on the south coast of North Uist, drowning pastures are visible now fragmented by repeated inundations and presenting the novel appearance at spring high tides of grass growing directly out of sea water! Along this stretch of coast may also be seen many tidal islets, some bearing the ruins of old houses, others the parallel ridges of plough or lazybed cultivation. Most of these are clearly too small, and now too awkward of access, to have been settled upon or cultivated in their present state. Clearly they were still attached to the main body of the land when they were so used and only subsequently, and relatively recently, cut off from it by the inexorable rise of the sea.

orogenesis » the formation of mountains

The continents, which form the upper part of the earth's crust, are made from elements which are of lesser density — and which therefore float upon — those of which the lower crust is composed. Deep within the earth thermal plumes are born. These are rising colums of hot molten matter. These rise from the interior up to the underside of the crust where they split up into opposed streams and, gradually cooling, they fall back towards the centre again. The friction of the plumes against the base of the crust forces the crustal plates, the tectonic plates, apart giving rise to the phenomenon of continental drift. It is clear, for example, that South America 'fits' into the west coast of Africa from which it was separated about 100,000,000 years ago.

When two plates collide — a very slow process — the edge of one slips below the other. The descending material is heated to melting point, at which time the lighter crustal matter rises up, under the edge of the static plate, lifting it above its original height. Meanwhile this edge has begun to crumple into the sharp ridges which we call mountain ranges. This process is presently taking place in the Himalaya, for example, where the Indian sub-continent is crashing into the Asian landmass and sinking beneath it. The upper parts of the mountain ranges retain their erstwhile geological character, i.e. if the rocks of the area were sandstones, the mountains are formed of folded sandstones. However, the underlying core of the mountains is completely metamorphosed, or changed, by the enormous temperatures and pressures involed.

These events took place along the east coast of the Western Isles during the Laxfordian and Scourian foldings in the remote past. Subsequent weathering has removed all but the core of the mountains thus formed, leaving low rounded hills where once great mountains towered.

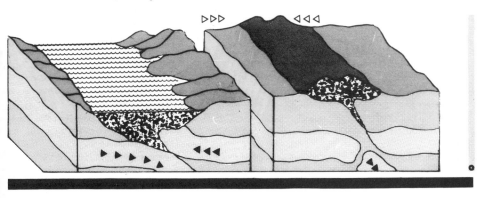

400000   300000   200000   100000

End of *ICE AGE* 12,000 yr's Bp ▶

This pasture land is being drowned by the rising sea.

In the islands south of Harris the surface of the Lewisian Gneiss slopes down very gently under the sea; its average slope is 1 in 250. If current estimates are correct and the sea has been rising at the rate of about 1m per 1000 years, then it must have risen some 5m (about 16ft) since the arrival of the first farmers on these islands. Given the shallow slope of the gneiss and a 5m rise in the sea level, it is easy to see that a strip of land up to 1.25km (roughly 1 mile) wide has been lost along parts of the west coasts of the islands south of Harris. In Harris, and indeed in Lewis also, the slope of the land into the sea is much steeper and so there has been little appreciable loss there. The rising sea has completed the segmentation of the islands, a process initiated by the ice sheets. It is interesting to note that a very small further rise will segment the islands to a far greater extent than has so far been achieved.

9000		6000		4000		2000	
Mesolithic		Neolithic		Bronze Age		Iron Age	

Not the least of the islands' many paradoxes is their relationship with the sea which destroys land but which also enriches the land to such an extent that settlement on the islands now is determined by the sea and access to it. Shell sand thrown up by the sea along the west coasts of the islands, mainly in the Uists and Benbecula, provides the richest and most fertile land in the West of Scotland. The extensive deposits of shell sand in the isles south of Harris make up a wide level plain called in Gaelic the *machair* (literally the plain). The sand overlies, in the main, till (mixed glacial deposits of clays, sands and stones), although in some areas it lies directly onto the gneiss. It is paradoxical, but uniquely Hebridean, that some of the earth's most recent geological deposits, the tills and the shell sand, rest directly on top of some of the earth's most ancient rocks.

Shell **sand** lying on **Gneiss**

The **encroachment** of the **sea**

All around the coasts of the Isles the evidence for the encroachment of the sea upon the land is visible. These illustrations show peat banks which are undergoing active erosion by the sea with isolated blocks of peat now cut off at high tide. Pastureland is also being inundated and water channels fragment this coastal pasture, at every tide.

THE THAW

AFTER THE ICE AGE

In terms of the vast areas of time in which geological events are usually measured, the end of the Ice Age was an abrupt affair which lasted — in all probability — just a few centuries! The cause of the great thaw is as obscure and poorly understood as the cause of the Ice Age itself, and one of the few things of which we can be sure is that it was not a final end to the Ice Age but merely the start of another interglacial. Interglacials are periods of relative warmth which have occurred sporadically throughout the Ice Age. Some have lasted as long, or longer than, the current example, while others have been very brief indeed.

Up to quite recently it was believed that the Ice Age consisted of four major episodes, during which the advancing ice sheets covered northern Europe. These glacial periods were separated by lengthy interglacial periods. This rather simple view was in part created by the fact that each successive readvance of the ice removed or buried most of the evidence for the earlier glacial and interglacial periods. The analysis of cores from the sea bed, undisturbed by the ice sheets, has shown that the picture is altogether more complex than we had imagined. The isotope of oxygen called 018 exists in nature in a proportion to the 'normal' 016 which is determined by temperature. By measuring the 018/016 ratios at successive levels of the sea cores it is possible to reconstruct — in outline — the temperatures prevailing during the life times of the microscopic creatures whose remains (which blanket the sea bed) provide the substance of the cores. The sea core analysis show that more than twenty periods occurred when the temperatures rose and the advance of the ice must have been halted, however briefly.

The present interglacial period known as the Flandrian interglacial seems typical of the major interglacial periods. It can be viewed as consisting of four phases. During the first (or Cryocratic) phase the rising temperature melts the ice and encourages the development of a tundra-type landscape. Here lichens, mosses and grasses replace each other in dominance as both climate and soils improve. The second phase (the Protocratic) is transitional with park tundra or tree-studded tundra becoming gradually filled in with trees. In the third phase (the Mmesocratic) the best climate of the interglacial period is achieved. This, the climatic optimum occurred around 3500 B.C. in the present interglacial (see information box on radiocarbon dating). In this phase forest cover (of deciduous trees in southern Britain, birch and pine in the north) becomes established. The soils are greatly improved in this process, becoming forest-brown-earths, the most fertile type to occur in Britain. The fourth and final phase

Mesolithic   10,000   9,000   8,000   7,000   6,000   5,000   4,

begins with the cooling of the climate, associated with greater rainfall. Tree cover
removed or destroyed in this phase is no longer replaced. Acidification of the soils
leads either to their podzolisation, if they are free draining, or their gleying if poorly
drained: both processes which impoverish the soils and both leading, ultimately, to the
formation of blanket or climatic peat.

GNEISS QUARRY (S.Uist)

The Highlands and Islands seem now to be in the final phase of this, the Flandrian interglacial. How much time remains to us we do not know, but clearly the outer isles will be amongst the first areas to feel the impact of any climatic worsening. In this respect events in the isles during 'the Little Ice Age', the period roughly from 1550 to 1900 B.C. are of some interest. Climatic deterioration made this a time of dramatic and occasionally catastrophic change. The island of Baleshare was sundered from North Uist one stormy night. Some townships like one on the west of Baleshare were lost to the sea, while elsewhere the movement of sand — at the Udal and Newton Ferry, for example — caused the resiting of whole townships and probably the destruction of others. In general, the effect of this 'Little Ice Age' was to reduce the length of the growing season, probably by as much as five or six weeks, and to reduce the upper limit of cultivation by 150m to 200m, i.e. by up to 600ft! The impact of this minor perturbation on the already precarious economies of the Highlands and Islands may easily be imagined and indeed may go some way to explaining the social unrest in these areas during this period.

WEathERED CoastliNE , , LEWis

Mesolithic	10,000	9,000	8,000	7,000	6,000	5,000	4

PØLLEN ANALySiS

Flowering plants produce pollen, in their anthers, and this forms the 'male' contribution in the fertilization process of the plant. The shell of each pollen grain is made of a material called sporopollenin which is extraordinarily resistant to decay. Pollen from different types of plants can be identified on the basis of their shape, organisation and surface sculpting, but in many cases it is only possible to identify the pollen to family or genus level. Thus while pollen of oak or wood sorrel can be readily identified, the pollen of all the grasses must be grouped together because the pollen of the hundreds of grass species are too closely similar to be readily distinguished from each other. The groups of plants that are identified in pollen analysis are called taxa (singular: taxon), and some contain single species, some whole families of plants.

Each year flowering plants produce pollen, often in great quantities, and their combined product contributes to the 'pollen rain', the mixture of pollen grains which, carried in the air, finally fall on a particular site. The pollen rain on any specific area represents three vegetational components: the local (within a few metres of the sample spot), the extra local (within a few hundred metres of the sample spot) and the regional. The last may include the pollen of species hundreds of miles distant; indeed pollen from coniferous trees, which is specially equipped for distribution by air currents, has been found at the North and South Poles!

When the pollen rain falls on a lake or a peat bog it becomes trapped on the wet surface and is, sooner or later, incorporated into either the lake sediments or the developing peat. Thus year after year the pollen rain is laid down in successive layers. In practice there is always some little admixture of the surface deposits so that the pollen of, say, 50 to 100 years becomes intermixed. However, the rate of vegetational change is invariably slow so that the loss of precision is not too important. If, then, the sediments of peats are sampled, usually be removing a cylindrical core of material, and dividing into successive slices, the pollen content of each slice can be extracted and identified. By graphing the relative proportions of the different pollen taxa (see example below) it is possible to reconstruct the vegetational history of an area.

TyPiCAL 'PeaT LakE

Abrupt changes in the diagram are sometimes observed. These usually show a sudden decline in the pollen of forest trees, an increase in grasses and herbs, possibly the appearance of cereal pollen, and an increase in the pollen of

4,000   3,000   2,000   1,000   bc 0 ad   1,000   1500 1700

some trees like hazel and birch. These events can be interpreted as follows: human settlers arrive and clear an area of woodland (decline in tree pollen) to provide fields for tillage (possibly deposition of cereal pollen). Grasses and herbs grow in the uncultivated parts of the clearing (increased pollen of these taxa), and eventually trees which form the under story of the forest (usually birch or hazel) can flourish on the margin of the clearing since they are no longer competing for light with the forest trees (hence the increase in pollen of these taxa).

By these means it is possible to reconstruct not only the natural development of the local vegetation but also to identify the intrusive presence of man.

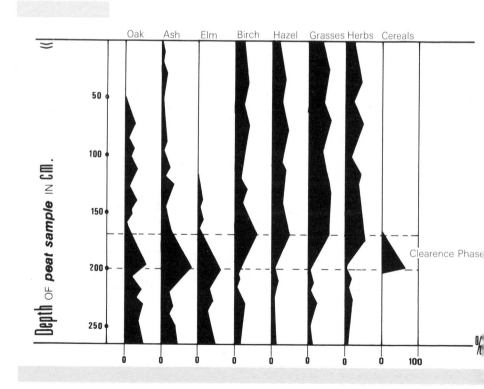

Palaeoecology is the study of the changes which have taken place in the natural environment in the past. The most important technique for reconstructing the changing vegetation in an area since the end of the Ice Age is pollen analysis which is described on pages 15–16. On the basis of pollen analysis undertaken up to recently in the Western Isles it was believed that woodland had never truly become established in the Isles. This was however at odds with firmly held local beliefs. Crofters pointed to the common discoveries of tree stumps and timber in peat cuttings and the readily observable tree stumps revealed at low tide, for example at Pabbay or near Sithean on Benbecula. The carbonised remains of wood of alder, willow, popular, pine and oak have been identified from sites excavated in the Isles.

It is of course always possible that some of these, especially the oak, were either wrongly identified or introduced to the Isles as parts of artefacts or boats or the like. However, it is improbable that all of the occurrences can be so dismissed, particularly when it is recalled that the present 'treelessness' of the Isles is more apparent than real, as we shall see. Finds of wild cat and blackbird from an Iron Age site, on Lewis, excavated in 1936, also suggest the existence of woodland even at that late date. Similarly the identification of the shells of snails of woodland habitats, by Dr. Evans, from Neolithic sites at Northon, Lewis and the Udal in North Uist again demonstrates the presence of woodland.

Thus it was not entirely surprising that recent pollen analyses from Tab nan Leobag near Callanish have contradicted the idea that the Isles have always been treeless. Rather, the conventional interglacial development was noted with a gradual transition from vegetation of Arctic and Alpine type to forest cover where birch and pine predominated and where even oak and elm may have grown. The demise of the woodland came early in the Western Isles, hardly surprisingly given their extremes of exposure and latitude, and it is probable that the woodland was being replaced by blanket peat between 2000 and 100 B.C. The ecology of the Isles has not, in all probability, changed very much since then. In describing the present vegetation of the Isles, therefore, we are describing its state since the Middle to late Bronze Age, through the Iron Age, Early Christian, Viking and Medieval periods. Its probable state in the earlier periods, the Neolithic and Early Bronze Ages, is described in Chapters 3 and 4.

As Sir Frank Fraser Darling has long since noted, 'the Outer Hebrides are not treeless, nor need they continue to be so desperately short of trees as they are'. Several fine stands of introduced trees

4,000 3,000 2,000 1,000 bc 0 ad 1,000 1500 1700

may be seen throughout the Isles, ranging in size and character from the large deciduous wood planted round Stornoway Castle by Lady Mathieson, to the small coniferous plantations of the Forestry Commission on North Uist. In general trees grow, and flourish, where they are protected from the wind and from grazing, usually by sheep. The impact of the wind on tree growth may be imagined when it is realised that up to 378 hours of gale-force (33 knot) or stronger winds have been recorded for the Butt of Lewis in the month of January. One of Lady Mathieson's plantations, of larch and conifers near Achmore, grew to maturity but was blown down in a gale in March 1921. The blasted stunted trees to the windward of the plantation at Newton in North Uist bear forceful testimony to the power of the Atlantic wind. Apart from these introduced trees there are remnants of older woods surviving in the sheltered areas of the Isles. The birchwood at Allt Volagin in South Uist is one such, but they are in general small, isolated and difficult of access. Difficulty of access is precisely what has preserved the scrub cover visible on virtually every islet which the sheep cannot reach in the myriad lakes of the islands. Birch, willow, alder and elder are common, while on the islands in Loch Druidbeg in South Uist a much wider range of species may be seen, including Scots Pine and some introduced species like Rhododendron.

Apart from the tree cover the islands' vegetation is interesting if somewhat impoverished, as island assemblages usually are. Lewis and Harris, the richest, floristically, of the chain, possess some 480 species, while mainland areas like the central Highlands can boast 850. The bulk on the island landscape is peat-covered and the sphagnum mosses, sedges, grasses and heather abound. In strong contrast the vegetation of the

Cotton grass.

WHiTE ORCHiDs

White Water Lillies.

Heather.

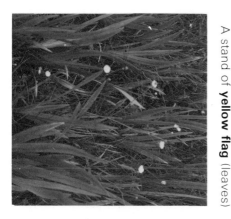

A stand of **yellow flag** (leaves)

GRaSSeS

coastal machair is a neutral grassland, in which flowers abound and orchids are common. Among the latter are the Common Spotted, the Early Marsh and the Lesser Butterfly Orchids. On the cultivated soils of the machair, rye and oats are the most traditional crops together with the primitive barley type known as 'bere'. Vegetables are grown in small numbers and of restricted range, mostly for local domestic consumption.

If the range of plants on the Isles seems restricted, the range of mammals, excluding the domesticated types, of course, is even more restricted. Again Lewis and Harris appear richest with some 15 species, in comparison with the mainland's 38. However, even the 15 species currently there are not all truly original to the Isles. The hedgehog, frog and mink are all recent introductions. The rabbit is less recent but nonetheless also introduced. Ferrets were released to try to control the rabbits, in Harris, and of course the feral cat is merely the descendant of domesticated animals which has reverted to nature. Similarly, the mountain hare was introduced, at Rodil, Harris in 1859, as was the brown hare, though the latter did not succeed in establishing itself. The date of introduction of the field mouse and the vole is not known but many zoologists believe them to have been Viking introductions. The Norwegian brown rat probably reached the Outer Isles in the eighteenth century, and it has succeeded in replacing the native black rat everywhere except in the Schiant Isles. In practice, then, of the land mammals only the red deer and the pygmy shrew can be confidently accepted as original citizens of the Isles. To these perhaps can be added the pine martin, which became extinct in the 1880s and, perhaps, the true wild cat, if its identification from an early (1936) excavation is to be accepted.

4,000   3,000   2,000   1,000   bc 0 ad   1,000   1500   1700

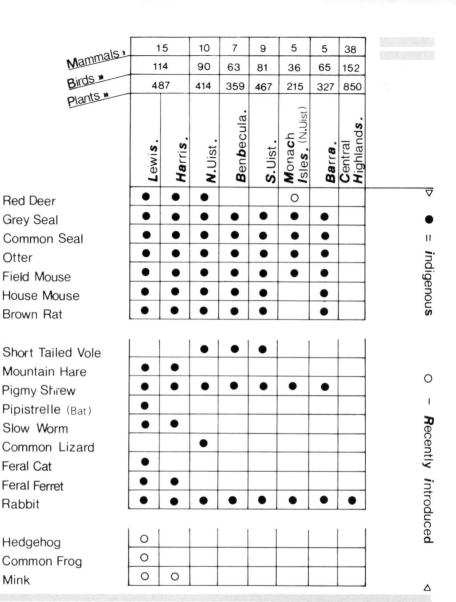

	Lewis	Harris	N.Uist	Benbecula	S.Uist	Monach Isles (N.Uist)	Barra	Central Highlands
Mammals »	15	10	7	9	5		5	38
Birds »	114	90	63	81	36		65	152
Plants »	487	414	359	467	215		327	850
Red Deer	●	●	●			○		
Grey Seal	●	●	●	●	●	●	●	
Common Seal	●	●	●	●	●	●	●	
Otter	●	●	●	●	●	●	●	
Field Mouse	●	●	●	●	●	●	●	
House Mouse	●	●	●	●	●		●	
Brown Rat	●	●	●	●	●		●	
Short Tailed Vole			●	●	●			
Mountain Hare	●	●						
Pigmy Shrew	●	●	●	●	●	●	●	
Pipistrelle (Bat)	●							
Slow Worm	●	●						
Common Lizard			●					
Feral Cat	●							
Feral Ferret	●	●						
Rabbit	●	●	●	●	●	●	●	●
Hedgehog	○							
Common Frog	○							
Mink	○	○						

(After R.J. Berry, 1979, "The Outer Hebrides : where genes & geography meet".)

● = indigenous

○ = Recently introduced

The isolation of the Isles, their distance from the mainland and the absence of any late- or post-glacial landbridges connecting them with the mainland may explain why they have such a very restricted natural fauna. Another possibility must be borne in mind, however, and that is that the Isles have undergone such considerable environmental changes that the original species, like the pine martin, were wiped out. Thus only species commensal with man were introduced or perhaps reintroduced to fill the available space.

Mesolithic   10,000   9,000   8,000   7,000   6,000   5,000   4,000

It is now generally accepted that the first hominids similar to modern man appeared in Europe sometime between 40,000 and 30,000 years ago. They arrived in Britain during this period, and they, and their flint axes and tools, have been recovered from sites in England and to a lesser extent in Wales. In Scotland, however, we have no evidence for these Palaeolithic (or Old Stone Age) settlers. As noted above, this may reflect no more than the fact that the later, and most severe, glacial periods have removed or destroyed the evidence of their existence. These people, the 'cave men' of popular literature, lived in close association with the herds of animals such as bison and horse which grazed the tundra on the edge of the ice sheets. Like the Plains Indians of the American Wild West, they seem to have been able to provide for almost all of their needs with animal products: flesh for food, skins for clothing, tenting, canoe coverings, etc, sinews for thread, thonging etc, bone for tools, hafts, etc. This fine balance of supply and demand was dislocated when the steadily improving climate encouraged the growth of forests. These split up the landscape and drove out or exterminated the herd animals of the open tundras and grasslands. Man was forced to adapt to this changed and changing environment; to hunt single prey, to use wood where bone had been employed before, to diversify his food sources and to exploit vegetable foods, nuts and fruits to compensate for the disappearance of the abundant herd animals. The period during which the resulting hunter/gatherer society emerged and flourished is called the Mesolithic period (or Middle Stone Age). In Scotland this began about 10,000 B.C. and continued until the introduction of farming, in the Neolithic period (New Stone Age), after which it was gradually supplanted or absorbed into the new economic system.

Some 5000 years have passed since the end of the Mesolithic Period proper, and the landscape of Britain has undergone enormous changes since then. The reader will not be surprised to learn that, in consequence, there are very few known sites of Mesolithic date in Scotland. Although the bulk of the Scots sites lie on the Ayrshire/Argyllshire coasts and in the inner Hebrides, no clearly Mesolithic site is recorded from the Outer Isles. There are two possible reasons for this. The first is that the surviving Mesolithic land surface in the Isles is now cloaked beneath either peat or shell sand and any sites which may exist are simply not visible. There is a second possible reason. Most of the known Scottish sites are located on or near raised beaches (see Chapter 1), and the occurrence of Mesolithic sites beside the — then — sea is a common phenomenon. In the Western Isles, however, there are no raised beaches and, as we have seen, the sea level has risen continuously since the end of the Ice Age. Thus the Mesolithic coastline is now drowned and lies, in places on the west coast, more than 1.5km offshore.

The occurrence of some of Scotland's largest Mesolithic sites in the Inner Hebrides, on Oronsay and Jura for example, makes it almost certain that the Outer Isles were also inhabited at this time. In this case the absence of evidence cannot be taken as evidence of absence! A somewhat more direct indication of the presence of Mesolithic man may be deduced from the evidence for woodland clearance just before 5000 B.C., which is enshrined in the pollen record from an area called Tob-nan-Leobag near Callanish, Lewis. The decline in the numbers of birch pollen and the presence of charcoal in the peat at the dated level suggest some clearance of the woodland, possibly by deliberate burning. It is argued that this practice was designed to ¡create grazing

clearings in the woodland to which game, especially red deer, would be attracted, and where they could be more easily trapped. In general, then, we may be quite confident that the Isles were inhabited, with a settled, resident community in the Mesolithic period, before 5000 B.C. and possibly several millennia later.

Mesolithic man has been described as a hunter/gatherer, and all of the excavated evidence supports this view of his life style and economy. He seems to have lived in camp sites which were seasonally occupied and which were so located, within the occupied territory, as to take advantage of the seasonally abundant food sources. Thus riverline and coastal sites may have been mainly occupied during the spring and summer to exploit the return to Scottish waters of schools of fish such as the saithe or, indeed, the salmon. Excavation of major Mesolithic sites on Oronsay has shown that saithe were harvested annually as their shoals passed among the islands. This information was derived from a study of otoliths, small bones from within the ears of the fish. At other sites animal bones and fruits or nuts indicate that they were also seasonally occupied. One such is the famous site at Star Carr in Yorkshire. The remains from this site were preserved in a peaty deposit which ensured the survival of bone and wood and other vegetable matter, substances which very rarely survive on sites of such great antiquity. The antlers of red and roe deer and of elk were recovered from this site, the bulk still attached to all or part of the frontlets of the animals' skulls. The remainder were examples which had been shed naturally — an annual event in the life times of these animals. We know from studies of modern deer and elk that the fully grown antlers of the red deer, for example, are present in the winter and shed in the spring, usually in April. From this it may

be deduced that the site at Star Carr was occupied during the winter and spring. In practice other factors continue to confirm this suggestion, and the seasonability of the site is established beyond reasonable doubt.

Apart from the fact that the sites were the seasonally occupied homes of hunter/ gatherers, we know very little of what they must have looked like or how they functioned. Evidence for houses, for example, is almost entirely lacking. Most sites are of the type called 'middens' and seem to be, as their name implies, refuse heaps consisting of food debris — usually sea-shells — in which stone or bone tools are also found. Only rarely is any evidence of a structure found, and even then it is usually difficult to interpret or reconstruct. A typical example is provided by the site near the river Lussa on the east coast of Jura. There three abutting rings of stone which average just over 1m in internal diameter were found. Charcoal from within the rings has been dated to just before 6000 B.C. These rings may in fact be hearths, but of any surrounding or enclosing structure no evidence was discovered. This has led to the belief that the settlements were camp sites, comparable with sites which are used by modern primitive peoples. However, it is hard to see how our Mesolithic forebears might have survived the rigours of our northern climes in tents and shelters suited to tropical or near tropical climates!

Recent work in Northern Ireland, at the site of Mount Sandel, in Co. Derry, has revealed the presence there of large wooden huts, some 6m in diameter, with central hearths. These have been dated to the period between 7000 and 6000 B.C., and are rather more like the kind of settlement which we might expect to find. Given the existence of substantial settlements of this type, how then ought we to view the midden sites and similar

Mesolithic   10,000   9,000   8,000   7,000   6,000   5,000   4,000 seasonal sites? These may be envisaged, in the traditional way, as sites seasonally occupied to exploit local food abundancies, by people who came from, and later returned to, a relatively permanent base camp of the Mount Sandel type. Thus the absence of convincing habitations at the largely coastal, seasonal sites is readily explicable.

So we can suggest, for the Western Isles, that Mesolithic man settled there, that he probably occupied permanent or semi-permanent sites like Mount Sandel, from which parties went out to seasonal sites, like the Oronsay or Jura sites, to exploit seasonally abundant food supplies such as fish or shellfish. The latter, especially where they were coastal, are probably now beneath the sea, whilst the inland examples may yet await discovery beneath the sands and peats of the Isles.

These people used stone, bone and antler as well as wood, which rarely survives, for their tools and equipment. The stone tools predominate, and they are usually made by chipping flint — a glassy stone — to shape. Occasionally in the West of Scotland other suitable local stone-types were used. The most important of these are Pitchstone, from Arran, Bloodstone (which is green) from Rhum and metamorphosed mud stones from Lewis. The Mesolithic period is divided into two, the Earlier and Later Mesolithics on the basis of the types of chipped stone tools in use. In general these were microliths, 'small stones' used either singly, as arrowheads for example, or in groups to provide composite or barbed tools or weapons. The Earlier Mesolithic types were broader and less rigidly geometrical in shape than the Later Mesolithic microliths. Of course not all the tools or weapons were made of microliths. Large flint axes, made razor sharp by the removal of transverse flakes parallel with the cutting edge, also occurred. Large implements in stone were also used, like the doughnut-shaped perforated maceheads and short cylindrical stone clubs, sometimes called 'limpet hammers'. Antler splinters were carved to form harpoon heads. These were up to 0.35m long with barbs carved along one or both edges. Antler was also used to make picks and mattocks.

It seems strange to discuss, as we have done here, the culture and economy of a people of whom these Outer Isles preserve no tangible remains, and yet, however slender the thread of the evidence may be, there can be no doubt that the Isles were occupied during this time. It may well also be that the first significant fragmentation of the island group occurred at the time of the change from Earlier to Later Mesolithic (about 6000 B.C.), since this was also the time of the major post-glacial rise in sea level. England was finally cut off from the Continent with the expansion and deepening of the North Sea. Trawlers occasionally dredge up Mesolithic implements from the sea bed between the east coast and Denmark. One such antler point from the Leman and Ower Banks has been dated to 6500 B.C. If no evidence for Mesolithic survives in the Outer Isles, the same cannot be said for the practice of using camps to exploit the seasonal harvesting of the sea. As we shall see, the use of seasonal sites survived the introduction of farming and continued in use at least until the Bronze Age and probably later.

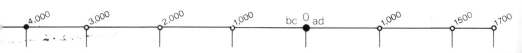

4,000   3,000   2,000   1,000   bc 0 ad   1,000   1500 1700

HIGH SUMMER
CLIMATIC IMPROVEMENT AND THE ARRIVAL of THE FIRST FARMERS

Throughout the Mesolithic period the natural environment of the Western Isles improved steadily. Shrubs and bushes had replaced the grasslands and were themselves replaced, in turn, by the spread of trees and the development of forest cover. Birch and Pine would have been the main constituents of forests at the latitudes and oceanic exposure of the Western Isles, but some authorities argue that even Oak and Elm became established in the Isles. One of the major difficulties in establishing the nature of the environment at the end of the Mesolithic period, and subsequently, is the fact that pollen rain (see Chapter 2) falling on the Isles may not represent the vegetation of the Isles properly. No land mass lies near enough, to the west, to contribute pollen, and the prevailing winds come from that direction. The islands are narrow, east to west, and so much of the locally produced pollen is whisked away to fall in the sea or on the mainland.

Thus we may only be seeing an extremely localised picture of the environment from any single sample spot. What is needed, clearly, is many more analyses but, first, and more importantly, a proper study of the nature and representativeness of the modern pollen rain. Enough evidence survives to allow us to envisage the landscape at that early date, however imprecisely. The knock-and-lochan character of the Isles imposed by the geological skeleton would, of course, have been much in evidence. However, instead of peat-brown, cold lochs scattered amongst peat-covered hills we may envisage stands of wood on the hills and slopes and clear water ponds and lakes, the reed-fringed haunts of fowl and heron. The islands were also substantially wider, as we have seen, possibly extending a kilometre or more further to the west where now the Atlantic rolls. Fish would, of course, have abounded in these early seas, some resident, some in transit on their annual migrations. The woods and forest bred red deer, significantly larger and more robust than the poor creatures who now gambol on the treeless peaty wastes. Seals were available, in season, and we know from finds of whale bones on sites of the period that whales were beached occasionally.

Neolithic   10,000   9,000   8,000   7,000   6,000   5,000   4,000

The islands must have seemed to flow
with milk and honey then, but they were
rather thinly spread. The bulk of the food
sources were seasonal and, while this
facilitated the hunter-gatherer traditions
of the Mesolithic, it did not allow for the
development of large or numerous,
settled communities. For this something
extra was needed, and that something
was farming. The improved climate and,
especially, the development of tree cover
had greatly improved the soils, which
were of the type called Forest-Brown
Earths, a type no longer to be found in
the Isles. Although peat certainly existed
then, it was restricted to wet hollows
and similar areas, and the bulk of the
land surface was available for
agriculture. The machair, as it now
exists, either did not exist at all or it lay
further west on land now drowned. This,
then, was the land into which the
earliest farmers moved, heralding the
new era, the Neolithic, or New Stone
Age, Period.

Farming, both animal herding and
arable cultivation, was invented or
developed in the area called the Fertile
Crescent, on the eastern shores of the
Mediterranean sea. It is difficult to give a
precise date for its beginnings for two
reasons. The first is that sites excavated
recently seem to provide earlier and
earlier dates for its inception. The second
reason is that farming developed out of
the Mesolithic hunter/gatherer traditions
probably over a quite lengthy period and
possibly at slightly different rates, and
dates, in different areas. However, we
can be reasonably sure that the
development of farming took place
sometime during the period 6000 to
8000 B.C.

It is easy to see that the capture of
animals is a logical development of
hunting them. Perhaps young animals
were captured when their mothers were
killed and, later, bred to produce a
readily available food supply. By
selective breeding desired traits could be
enhanced. Docility in cattle as well as
high milk yields are characteristics of the
domesticated animals, and it is certain
that these were achieved deliberately by
selective breeding. Some characteristics
seem to have been acquired as accidents
or byproducts of domestication, amongst
which the shortening of the snout of the
domesticated pig is probably the most
remarkable, and the development of
wool on sheep the most useful.

Similarly the impetus to arable
agriculture may be seen as a logical
extension of food gathering. Its
beginnings need have been no more than
the erection of a fence to prevent wild
animals from grazing natural
concentrations of food plants. From
there it is but a short step to extending
such natural concentrations by
transplanting; and only a short step more
to full tillage. Undoubtedly there were

many false starts but, in time, regimes suited to particular soils and areas were evolved. The purely Mesolithic hunter/gatherers must have coexisted with the emerging farmers for long periods, but eventually the efficiency of farming ensured the success of the settled and expanding farm communities, and Mesolithic man was gradually absorbed into the Neolithic way of life.

Farming began in the Fertile Crescent because of the unique occurrence there of the necessary conditions together with the wild forebears of all the domesticated animals and of wheat and barley. The 'muflan', the ancestor of both sheep and goats, occurred there, together with cattle, pigs, horses and dogs. All of these, except the muflan, also existed in Europe and in parts of Britain though not in the Western Isles. Einkorn and emmer, the ancestors of wheat and barley, however, did not exist in Europe. The practice of agriculture spread rapidly across Europe from the Near East, probably reaching the British Isles partly overland via Central and Northern Europe, and partly by the sea route, across the Mediterranean and up the Atlantic seaboard.

| Neolithic | 10,000 | 9,000 | 8,000 | 7,000 | 6,000 | 5,000 | |

The date of the arrival of the earliest farmers in Scotland is, like so much else, not precisely known. We do know that before 3000 B.C. they were sufficiently well established to begin building the great stone tombs by which they are chiefly known. But how long it took them to become so well established is simply unknown at present. Up to quite recently it was believed that they arrived at just about 3000 B.C. because many, if not all, pollen analyses showed a massive clearance of Elm at that date. However, the 'Elm Decline', as this feature came to be called, was simply too synchronous to be attributable to man. Over the great part of Northern Europe and the British Isles the Elm Decline took place in a very short time interval very close to 3000 B.C. Farming simply could not have spread that quickly over such a vast area. Dutch Elm disease, however, could, as we have learned to our cost in the past decade or two, and it is probable that some such disease was responsible for the Elm Decline.

At about the same time as archaeologists began to suspect the nature of the Elm Decline, a number of pollen analyses began to emerge of which pre-Elm Decline clearances were a feature. These were, in general, attributed to Mesolithic activities such as forest burning to create game clearings. However, some of these analyses also turned up cereal pollen at the level of the early clearances. Since there are no cereals native to these islands — the British Isles — these pollen grains represent incontrovertible evidence for the presence of farming communities, even though the communities themselves have not yet been located. It is thus probable that farming arrived in Britain not later than 4000 B.C., and possibly even earlier than that.

It is not in fact true to say that none of these early Neolithic farmsteads has been found. At least one has; this is the great timber hall at Balbridie near Crathes in Aberdeenshire. This magnificent structure measured 26m by 13m wide and is now represented only by the post holes in which the massive wall posts were set. It has been radiocarbon dated to the period 3800 to 3600 B.C. This site is clearly Neolithic, because masses of carbonised cereal grains were found in the tops of the post holes and in pits within the structure. Several similar sites are now known which may, on excavation, prove to be of the same order of date. Like Balbridie, these were believed to be Dark Age Halls (or Palaces).

The discovery of both early clearance phases, in pollen analyses, and of relatively early house structures in Northern Ireland suggests that the Neolithic had extended even into the northern latitudes of the British Isles well before 3000 B.C. In the absence of pollen of cereals it is not possible to suggest that the early clearance, about 5000 B.C. in the pollen analyses from Tob na Leobag, Callanish, Lewis, is evidence for Neolithic settlement. It is, after all, fully 1000 years earlier than the earliest known Neolithic dates for Scotland. Until further evidence is to hand, then, it is probably best to conclude that this particular episode is of Mesolithic origin, and to assume that farming did not arrive for another 1500 to 2000 years.

One of the major recent debates in archaeology has centred on whether new social and economic systems are introduced by invading — or at least intruding — people or by the diffusion of ideas. Did Neolithic settlers actually arrive on the Western Isles, complete with their animals and seedstock, or did the idea of farming gradually seep northwards with the residents of each area trading with that south of them for seed and animals? On balance one feels that the required knowledge was so new and so 'different', and the Isles so remote, that some actual movement of people was necessary, at least in this instance. They need have come from no further than Skye, of course, or the adjacent mainland. It is believed that they used skin-covered boats like the currachs which are still in use on Ireland's western seaboard. Although flimsy and apparently fragile, these were regularly used to ferry cattle and sheep to the Blasket and Arran islands over seas every bit as difficult and dangerous as the Minch

The passage grave **at** Barpa Langass

Neolithic   10,000   9,000   8,000   7,000   6,000   5,000

The Mesolithic midden sites on Oronsay have been radiocarbon dated to the period just before 3000 B.C., while Mesolithic sites on Jura are dated to 2500 to almost 2000 B.C. The interesting thing about these dates is that they are so much later than the earliest dates from known Neolithic sites. This suggests that either Mesolithic hunter/gatherers continued in being long after farming was introduced, and independently of the farmers, or alternatively, that the dependence of the farmers on hunting, fishing etc was such that seasonal camps continued in use. In the latter event either the farmers themselves used the midden site or, perhaps, the descendants of the Mesolithic settlers used them, trading their catches for farm produce. Relationships like the latter have been observed amongst modern primitive peoples. There is no reason to suspect that the Neolithic people exterminated the Mesolithic communities, which pre-existed them in the Outer Hebrides. The evidence from the Inner Hebrides suggests that the latter were either absorbed into the Neolithic economy or alternatively found it possible to coexist with their Neolithic neighbours.

Between 3000 and 2000 B.C., and usually closer to the latter date, there began in Scotland the building of megalithic or great-stone tombs. These have come to represent the Neolithic period to such an extent that one might be forgiven for believing that the land was populated by the dead rather than the living. The megaliths usually consist of a buried chamber of some sort over which an enormous cairn of stones has been erected. They are commonly sited on hills or on hill slopes and are now highly visible in the midst of the heather-covered moorland. The ordinary houses of the period were almost certainly built of wood and, after their abandonment and decay, only the post holes below ground level remain to betray their earlier existence. When the ground is later covered in up to 2m of peat it is all but impossible to locate the settlements. Accidental discovery or their uncovering by coastal erosion occasionally reveals Neolithic houses, and excavation at the Udal, North Uist and Northton in Harris of coastal erosion sites has revealed settlements of late Neolithic date. Against these two, however, the Outer Isles can boast some 29 or 30 megalithic tombs, so it is hardly surprising that the archaeology of the dead outweighs the archaeology of the living for the Neolithic period.

The megalithic tombs are of two basic types, each of which has many variants. Passage grave is the name applied to those which consist of a chamber entered by a passage and set within a circular cairn the edge of which is defined by a kerb of large stones. The passage leads out to the kerb which is usually indented at the point where they meet. In small, roughly circular cairns the internal kerb, at the entrance, can give the cairn a kidney-shaped plan. Where the inturn of the kerb is less severe, the cairn may appear heel-shaped.

The gallery graves constitute the second major divison of the megalithic tombs. These usually consist of a single relatively long chamber which is subdivided by sills — stones set on edge across the floor of the chamber — or by pairs of jamb stones — upright slabs set onto the side walls, at right angles, in opposed pairs. These are normally set in long cairns which may be trapezoidal in shape, being higher and wider at the entrance and tapering to the rear. The length of these cairns, often in excess of 30m, rarely bears any relation to the lengths of the chambers they contain, which rarely exceed 10m. The entrance to these chambers may be emphasised by setting a facade of upright slabs (orthostats), tallest on either side of the entrance and reducing in height to the outer edges. The facade can be crescentic, with two 'horns' of the cairn projecting forward to embrace a forecourt area.

Two thirds of the chambered tombs of the Western Isles are in North Uist. Four of these have long cairns and fifteen circular cairns. It may be assumed that all fifteen are passage graves, although some of them are either unopened or so badly ruined that only excavation could confirm this assumption. Of the long cairns, it is not always certain that they are gallery graves, since in some cases circular cairns have been reshaped later by the addition of material, to make a long cairn. The visitor may discern this at sites like Barba nam Feannag, North Uist or, more readily, at Airidh na h-aon Oidhche, South Uist. Gallery graves do, of course, occur in the Isles, like the sites at Carinish or Clettraval on North Uist, but they are clearly in the minority; the bulk of the sites are passage graves

Neolithic   10,000   9,000   8,000   7,000   6,000   5,000

cairn at Barpa Carinish **with** Eaval rising on the skyline.

~~~~~

The general practice with these cairn seems to have been that the chamber was built within a cairn of its own. This was necessary to keep the corbels in place and allow for the completion of the roofing. Meanwhile, less skilled labour was used to fill in the cairn material between the kerb and the chamber with its cairn. In damaged or destroyed cairn it is sometimes possible to make out the line of this internal cairn. Please do not remove cairn stones to search for this, other features. The removal of even small amounts of material greatly weakens corbelled structures which rely on the weight resting on them for stability. This may seem paradoxical but it is none the less true (as a half hour's experimenting with a set of wooden blocks will demonstrate). Internal walls can also occur within cairns which have been enlarged or extended.

It has been suggested that some, or all, of these cairns have been constructed to precise plans using a standard unit of length and orientation in such a way as to indicate some significant astronomical event, such as sunrise or sunset at midwinter or midsummer. The Hebridean sites have their entrances set between south and east. It is possible that some of them, like the famous example at Newgrange in Ireland, are so organised that the rising sun at midwinter shines down their passages into the chamber. In general the claims for the precise use of a standard unit of length and of precise ground plans have been rejected. The evidence simply could not sustain them. Similarly, claims for the use of megalithic sites as very precise astronomical instruments have also been dismissed, but most students of the period accept now that orientation, in a less precise way, was practised.

The typical Hebridean passage grave has a relatively short passage, 2m to 3m long, and 1m wide, which gives access to a chamber which is circular (or nearly so) or elongated and which ranges in size roughly from 4m to 6m in diameter. The walls of the entrance can be made of orthostats alone (as at Unival) or dry stone walling (as at Barpa Langass), and are roofed with large stone lintel slabs. Similar techniques are used in the construction of the chambers. The chambers, if they were small enough, were roofed with slabs but more commonly by the use of corbelling. This is the deceptively simple technique of laying down successive courses of slabs so that each oversailed the course below it until the area to be covered could be sealed with a single slab. Usually, the lowest layer of corbels rested on the cairn material behind rather than the orthostats which formed the chamber walls.

In some gallery graves, notably at Midhowe in Orkney, low stone benches

Neolithic 10,000   9,000   8,000   7,000   6,000   5,000

held the articulated skeletons of the most recent burials, while the remainder of the tomb held the usual disarticulated mass of bones. In these examples the tombs may have served as ossuaries or charnel houses in which the bones of a tribe's or family's ancestors were stored. The tomb at Isbister in South Ronaldsay, Orkney, was exceptional in that the bones of eagle talons had been deposited with the human burials. John Hedges, who published the report on this marvellous site, has suggested that the eagle may have been the totem or sacred creature of the tribe buried there.

Pottery had been deposited with the bones at Unival, in all seventeen vessels, of which five were intact and a further nine largely so. The remaining three, however, were represented by a handful of sherds. It is possible that broken pots were removed from the tomb periodically, only the odd small sherd being overlooked. These vessels are of characteristic Neolithic type, round-bottomed with a sharply defined shoulder. It is probable that these vessels held tribal offerings to the dead, and modern scientific techniques can nowadays be employed to discover what their contents had been. Vessels from the older excavations have been handled too much and thus contaminated, and are unsuitable for such studies. Modern techniques may also help to overcome the problem of bone decay in the Western Isles' acid soils. From a chemical analysis of proteins surviving in the soil, even after all bone has decayed away, it has proved possible to identify the sex and approximate age at death of decomposed corpses. This technique has yet to be applied to chambered tombs but it seems to offer some hope for future studies.

It is clear that the chambers of the megaliths were used repeatedly, and radiocarbon dating suggests that they went on being used over many centuries. Indeed there is some indication that a thousand years could have passed between the erection of the tomb and its final closure. The small numbers of bodies represented by the surviving bones cannot represent all of the members, even of a single very small tribe over so lengthy a period of use. It is possible that only the remains of particular people were placed in the tombs, or that earlier remains were periodically removed and disposed of in some way. In either event it is hard to argue that the cairns functioned as simple tombs; clearly they had a greater significance than that. Each cairn sits in its own territory, separate from all the others, and it is probable that each belonged to a single tribe or group. The construction of even a small cairn required the cooperative efforts of a large part of the tribal group to which it belonged. The function of these tombs is a fascinating study. It may seen obvious that tombs functioned as burial places, but these tombs were clearly much more than simple graves. To begin with it must be noted that very few bones have survived in the Hebridean examples because the acidity of the soil water has dissolved them away in most cases. Some did survive in the site of Unival, North Uist, where part of the skeleton of a mature woman was found in a box-like arrangement of stones — a cist — on one side of the chamber. Her remains lay on, and were covered with, a mass of charcoal. Parts of other bones lay on the floor of the chamber, and ribs of a person less than twenty-one years old were also found in the cist.

In other sites of this type elsewhere in Scotland where bone is rather better preserved, as for example in Orkney, the burial practices can be better

Neolithic | 10,000 | 9,000 | 8,000 | 7,000 | 6,000 | 5,000 | 4,000

understood. They were exposed somewhere other than the tomb to allow all the flesh to decay. Then the bones were gathered up and deposited in the chambered cairn. In this process many bones, particularly the smaller ones, were often lost, and even where multiple burials, several in excess of one hundred, are placed in the chamber it is usually impossible to reconstruct even a single complete skeleton. This has given rise to the suggestion that the bones may have been repeatedly removed from the chamber to be used in some ritual and then replaced, with the degree of loss and damage increasing all the time. Repeated re-use of the tomb by the community together with the rituals which must have been associated with the insertion and removal of bones and bodies must have elevated the chambered cairn to the status of a cathedral. Indeed one wonders at times if its use as a centre and focus for the religious and group identity of the community, was its primary function and the matter of the bones it contains quite secondary. Religion, emotion, philosophies and ideas cannot be excavated, and those of our ancestors are as unknowable to the archaeologist as to any other person. In the final analysis the function of the tombs will always remain a matter for argument and discussion, and therein lies a great part of their charm.

In the Neolithic period, then, the Western Isles were a booming vibrant area, rich in the diversity of habitants and densely populated, for the first time. When, in the post-medieval period, the population again increased, it was in far less favourable circumstances. If the Isles had a golden age, the Neolithic period was that age, and its legacy to us, the megalithic tombs which survive in such large numbers, is a fine legacy indeed. Their neglected state and neglected study reflect poorly on us all.

THE RAINY SEASON ■

CLIMATIC DETERIORATION AND THE DEVELOPMENT of THE BRONZE AGE

4

The Neolithic period proper ended in Scotland sometime around 2000 B.C., with the introduction of metalworking settlers and the beginning of the Bronze Age. The introduction of the new technology seems to have been relatively painless but, eventually, the Bronze Age caused changes in the organisation of social and political life together with, or perhaps caused by, changes in the economic basis on a scale which was not to be repeated until the clearances of the recent and unhappy past. The Bronze Age in the Highland Zone (which includes the islands) can be considered in two distinct phases. The first of these can be viewed as a Late Neolithic/Early Bronze Age period in that the Neolithic communities, while continuing in existence, had grafted onto them probably new populations and certainly new religions and social practices introduced from outside. This period seems to have been as vigorous as the preceding Neolithic had been. However, it was taking place against a background of worsening climate, and sometime towards the middle of the second millennium B.C. (around 1500 B.C.) a dramatic change for the worse took place. The climate of all of northern Europe deteriorated, and in Scotland and the Western Isles in particular conditions became much wetter and much colder.

The impact of these changes on the landscape, as we shall see in detail below, was little short of disastrous for the inhabitants. The Late Bronze Age which followed was lived in a landscape completely different from that which had gone before. Peat had developed and

ChapteR

Bronze Age   10,000   9,000   8,000   7,000   6,000   5,000   4,000

was spreading over the hitherto arable areas, the hill lands became uninhabited, and settlement had to retreat from many marginal areas. By the end of the Bronze Age the landscape had assumed a form which was not significantly different from what we see now. It will come as no surprise to learn therefore that the all-embracing peat has largely swallowed the monuments of the Bronze Age in the Outer Isles. Large sites like the stone circles or the cairns of the Early period can still be seen above the peat, but of the houses, farms and fields nothing is seen until they are revealed in peat cutting or exposed in areas being eroded by the sea. It is necessary for this period, as for some others, to use the evidence from elsewhere in Scotland, particularly the west coast area, to help create a picture of what was happening in the Outer Isles.

4,000   3,000   2,000   1,000   bc 0 ad   1,000   1500   1700

Since the environmental changes in this period are of such importance, it is useful to consider these before discussing the nature of the Bronze Age itself. All major environmental change is ultimately caused by climate, or at least it was until recently when man's capacity to disrupt the natural order by industrial and other pollutants has completely changed the picture. Towards the end of the Neolithic period average temperatures decreased. This led to an extension southwards of the circumpolar wind systems which determine cloud movement etc. This forced the anticyclonic weather belt southwards in turn and greatly increased the volume of rainfall. As a result of this and also because world temperature was still falling, a considerable cooling then ensued. Thus, by the middle of the Bronze Age conditions were very wet and very cold. One of the prime indicators of climatic disruption in the Western Isles is the breakdown of the machair system and the movement of sand. It is clear from radiocarbon dated levels at the sites of Northton, Harris and Roshinish, Benbecula that while sand was being blown inland at the close of the Neolithic, the major sand movements took place just before the beginnings of the Bronze Age and continued throughout the period of its development. Like most climatic events, this deterioration would not seem abrupt to the islands' inhabitants, but although it may have been imperceptible in the course of their relatively short lifetimes, its effects were nevertheless cumulative and inexorable. Where the soils were free-draining, the increased precipitation leached vital minerals out of the upper layers and precipitated them in insoluble pans, or sheets, lower down in the soil. Here they were no longer available to growing plants, and they ultimately formed an obstacle to drainage. The land then became waterlogged, and unless something was done to relieve this, the development of peat ensued, sooner or later. This process of soil leaching is called 'podzolisation' and the resulting soils 'podzols'. *Podzolis* is a Russian word meaning grey soil and it is named from the leached layer which lies below the black peaty topsoil. In countless cuttings in the Western Isles the visitor will see colourful displays of podzols, especially where the grey leached layer beneath the black topsoil overlies a bright orange layer into which all of its iron salts have been washed.

Examination of such profiles will often reveal an iron pan at the bottom of the orange layer. This is a virtually continuous sheet of iron oxides or rust, cementing soil and stone together in an impermeable layer that blocks all drainage. While the cultivation of podzols is not impossible, it is very labour-intensive, and mounting evidence from Highland Scotland suggests that Bronze Age settlers gradually withdrew from upland and marginal areas in the face of the advance of podzolised soils.

Let us, for the moment, abandon the cold wet Late Bronze Age and return to the happier Early phase and consider the peoples who brought with them the new age. These people are known as the Beaker Folk, a name derived from the distinctive style of pottery which they produced. These Beaker Folk seem to have originated in the south of Spain soon after the middle of the second millennium B.C., and within a few centuries their distinctive pottery was being produced over a vast area which spreads from North Africa to Scandinavia and from Ireland to Poland. No other known social movement, including Christianity, spread so far so quickly. Two main reasons for their success are suggested, the first of which relates to the equipment which is often found in association with their pottery. This is the equipment of the archer. They produced

Bronze Age 10,000   9,000   8,000   7,000   6,000   5,000   4,000

tanged and barbed arrowheads of flint which are miniature masterpieces in themselves. Wristguards, rectangular plates of bone or soft stone, pierced at the corners to be mounted with a string on the archer's wrist to protect it from the lash of the bowstring are also found. Personal ornaments in gold and jet were also worn by the Beaker Folk. Thus it appears that their social organisation was based on the importance of the warrior; theirs may have been the first warrior aristocracy in Europe. It is also suggested that they were mounted warriors; indeed it is now believed that they reintroduced the horse to Ireland where it had become extinct. Their successful expansion, according to the first theory, is therefore explained by suggesting that the Beaker Folk were mounted warriors who, perhaps like the Huns, suddenly burst out of their homelands and expanded far and wide overcoming the indigenous Neolithic groups. They assumed control over Neolithic communities by the simple expedient of making themselves the village overlords. Thus relatively small numbers of invaders could control much larger numbers of subjects and by exploiting their native rivalries offset the possibility of organised and united revolt.

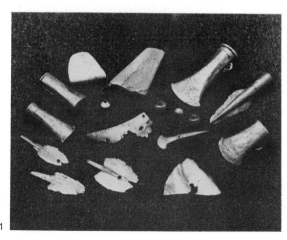

1

If this seems at first a little short of convincing, it would be well to remember that the Norman invasions of both Scotland and Ireland were conducted along these lines. The initial Roman conquest of Barbarian Europe followed a similar course; in allying themselves to native tribes, the Romans ensured that no united front or concerted effort ever faced them.

The second theory used to explain the success of the Beaker Folk relates to their pottery and its possible function. Over the past few years deposits from the insides of Beakers which have been found in burial deposits have been analysed, and these analyses suggest that the pots were used to hold alcoholic beverages, beers and meads. It has long been realised that the arrival of the Beaker Folk coincides with the introduction of barley, or at least with its planting on a large scale, wheat having been the main cereal crop of the Neolithic peoples. It has therefore been suggested that the spread of Beaker pottery is not due to an actual movement of large numbers of people but to the expansion of a semi-religious cult, a cult of intoxication. According to this theory, a religion, probably a mystical religion, grew up around the use of alcohol as an intoxicant in much the same way as tribes in Central America and the Southern USA used, and still use, peyote mushrooms which contain halucinogenic drugs as a means of experiencing a mystical communion. Thus it is suggested that the spread of Beaker pottery should be viewed as the spread of a religion or cult symbol, not necessarily the spread of a people. With much misgivings, but a hope of forgiveness, one is tempted to suggest that alcohol and religion still survive as potent forces in the life of the Outer Isles, though now happily sundered from each other.

Late Bronze age hoard

2

Bronze Age   10,000   9,000   8,000   7,000   6,000   5,000   4,000

Apart from the introduction of a new style of pottery, perhaps the most significant change introduced at this time was the change from multiple burials to single burial. It will be recalled that the bones of the Neolithic settlers were deposited, often in large numbers, in chambered tombs, after their bodies had been exposed elsewhere for the flesh to decay. In the Bronze Age individual burial was the norm. The bodies of the dead were first folded into a foetal position and placed in a cist, a box-like arrangement of stone slabs, usually set into the ground and often but not always covered with a cairn of stones or a mound of earth. The burial might be accompanied by Beaker pots or some of the other characteristically Beaker equipage, including the new metal in the form of bronze daggers or gold ornaments. It is clear that some of the cairns were used as small cemeteries and contained more than one cist. These are called multiple cist cairns. Sometimes also the cists occurred in groups, and more than one burial might be inserted into a cist, the second or succeeding burials some considerable time later than the first. It is probably that cists were marked in some way, perhaps by standing stones or pillars because in the absence of a covering cairn it is hard to see how their position could have been rediscovered and secondary burials inserted.

VIKING Tortoiseshell Broches   Viking Sword Hilt

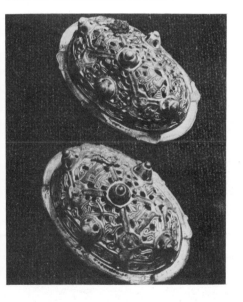  

4

The change from multiple burials, where all seemed equally treated, to single burials where some burials, especially those under cairns or containing elaborate ornaments or equipment, seem to demonstrate social ranking, is taken to indicate that there is a transition from an egalitarian type of society in the Neolithic to some form of oligarchy or government by the few in the Bronze Age. However, the common practice of inserting Bronze Age burials into Neolithic cairns without destroying the deposits of bone, etc already there suggests that the transition was a relatively peaceful one, with respect for the older tradition being shown by the practitioners of the new.

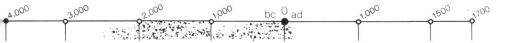

Short cists of Bronze Age type have been noted at Ruadha na Traghad, North Uist, and at Calvey Island, South Uist. One isolated cist and another within a cairn were discovered in the last century at Borve in Benbecula, while what appears to be a cist cemetery has been eroded out of the sand dunes at Traighe na Luibe on Boreray. It is probable that several of the large but uninterpretable cairns, such as those near Clachan, are of Bronze Age date, but only excavation will confirm this.

5

TYpical **Beaker** Assemblage

In time a local imitation of the true Beaker pottery began to emerge. This was compounded of Beaker-type ornament on vessels which were rather crude and thick in comparison with Beakers and which are of somewhat different forms (see data box). Its emergence coincided with the introduction of cremation, rather than inhumation, as the burial rite. Some of the Food Vessels, we know from radiocarbon dates, are much earlier than some of the Beaker burials, and this led in the past to suggestions that the Food Vessels were made by Neolithic survivors rather than by the Beaker Folk themselves. This seems less credible now that we realise that it is not necessary to envisage large-scale movements of people at the introduction of the Bronze Age. Food Vessels in turn gave way to Urns, very large vessels with improbable small bases. These were used to contain the cremated remains and were often inserted upside down in simple holes in the ground with no attempt at the construction of a cist.

The containment of the bones of a community was only one of the ways in which the Neolithic chambered tombs served their communities; as discussed above, they also and perhaps more importantly served as centres of religious observance. With the change to single burials widely distributed, this function could no longer be met by the burial sites, and was, we believe, taken over by the stone circles and the monuments called Henges. Examples of the latter type are unknown in the Highland Zone. That stone circles existed in the Neolithic period cannot be doubted, indeed the passage grave at Bryn Celli Ddu in Wales is built on top of a stone circle. Closer to home the passage graves at Clave south of Inverness are surrounded by stone circles which we have no reason to doubt are contemporary with them. However, it was during the Bronze Age that stone circles flourished, particularly during the early part of the period.

The Royal Commission (on Ancient and Historical Monuments) surveyors in 1928 listed twenty-one stone circles in the long island, and others have been discovered since. Amongst the latter, that at Achmore was discovered and partly excavated by the Ponting family of Callanish. The circles seem to occur in distinct concentrations, the foremost of which is a group of sites located around Loch Roag in Lewis. This contains the marvellous site of Callanish which is second only to Stonehenge in importance among the stone circles of Britain. Like the chambered tombs, stone circles sometimes contained burials, sometimes in association with Beaker pottery. Some types of circles, like the Aberdeenshire circles, surround cairns which in turn cover burial deposits. However, it is clear that this is a minor aspect of their function, perhaps not dissimilar to the burial in cathedrals of individuals outstanding for their piety, heroism or, latterly, simply for their wealth. It is generally accepted that they served as centres for the religious observances of communities which were being concentrated into areas of good land by the deterioration of the environment, and by the increased social organisation which is the keynote of the Bronze Age.

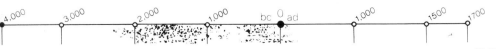

Much has been made of late of the possibility that these circles were presided over by highly sophisticated 'priests' who combined in themselves the considerable skills of civil engineering, mathematics, and astronomy. We are told that the circles are not truly circular, a fact which has not escaped us, but are rather constructed to precise geometric shapes, often of considerable complexity, and constructed using a standard unit of length with an accuracy to be measured in thousandths of an inch. Furthermore, it is said, the circles are so constructed that they serve as astronomical observatories facilitating observations of truly astounding complexity and of a precision which might well be envied by the modern astronomer. It has been shown to the satisfaction of all but the lunatic fringe that the geometry and precise metrology (measurements) are an illusion, created by a combination of poor research and the testing of naive hypotheses by inadequate and inappropriate statistical methods. Similarly the precision argued for in the laying out of astronomical sighting lines cannot be supported by the available evidence. This does not deny the existence of such settings, since their occurrence is too common to be purely coincidental. It does however suggest that these priests were not intellectual super-heroes, possessors of arcane and wonderful knowledge, which some would yet suggest they were. It cannot be pointed out too often that there is absolutely nothing else in the societies of the late Neolithic and Early Bronze Age which could be said to provide evidence for the existence of such a body of men, or indeed of such a body of knowledge.

Three settlements of the Early Bronze Age are known from the Western Isles: Northton in Harris, the Udal in North Uist, and Roshinish in Benbecula. All three were discovered in the course of excavations undertaken on coastal erosion sites. Northton and the Udal have both been the subjects of extensive excavations, particularly the latter which, some twenty years after its initiation, is still being excavated. When ultimately the information from these sites is published, it will greatly amplify and, no doubt, alter our understanding of settlements of the period. At Northton a simple oval had been cut into the sand which contained a central hearth and an arrangement of small post holes which the excavator interpreted as part of a light hut or perhaps a tent. The Beaker levels at this site had been radiocarbon dated to 1531 to 1654 b.c., and amongst other finds recovered from this site were two small combs which were probably used to make the comb-impressed patterns of decoration common to Beaker pottery. At Roshinish areas of cultivation were identified by the patterns of ard-marks which survived there. The ard is a simple stone-tipped wooden plough which is still in use in some areas of the world, and ard-marks are patterns of linear gouges left in the subsoil by the tip of the ard. Two areas of ard marking, separated by a shallow ditch, were interpreted by the excavator at Roshinish as two adjacent fields. The crops grown at this site were barley and wheat, and carbonised examples of both survive. The barley was clearly the dominant crop, as is anticipated from Bronze Age sites.

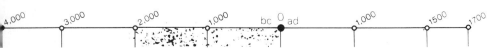

4,000   3,000   2,000   1,000   bc 0 ad   1,000   1500   1700

The Late Bronze Age is almost unrepresented in the Western Isles, or at least is not very visible there. The reason for this is the thick blanket of peat which covers everything. When the peat was cleared away from around the stones at Callanish, it was found to be over 1.5m deep. Its removal there revealed the chambered tomb at the centre of the monument which had been unknown and unsuspected until then. Similarly peat cutting at the site of Tob nan Leobag has revealed field walls and other structures of early date. Hut circles and field banks of possible Bronze Age date have been revealed, again in peat cuttings at Sheshader, Lewis, and few though these remains are, they serve to indicate that Late Bronze Age settlement in the Isles was larely similar to that elsewhere in the Highland Zone, where the evidence is more easily observable.

The hut circle is, par excellence, the monument of the Late Bronze Age. It consists of a pennanular (i.e. broken circle) bank of earth or, more commonly, stone, both averaging 6m to 8m in diameter, and that is all that usually survives to represent it. Excavations reveal however that large and relatively comfortable houses once stood on these sites. The conical roof was thatched, and its rafter ends rested directly on the enclosing bank. Internally the roof was further supported by a circle of wooden posts, the socket holes of which have been observed in excavation. Immediately inside the bank a ring of stakes or small posts sometimes carried screens of woven wattles. In one site excavated on the Isle of Arran these survived as charcoal where the house had burned down. On other sites, not only in Scotland but even as far away as Dartmoor, traces of this 'lining wall' have been identified.

Hut circles occur in significant groups or clusters of up to ten or twelve huts, often set within the remains of what appear to be field systems. Since both the huts and the field banks are usually multi-period, it is not always possible to reconstruct the form of these proto-villages, but it is clear that they do constitute village-type settlements. Those forces of environmental deterioration and social stratification which, it was argued above, lead to the concentration of settlement into favoured areas, found their logical culmination in the evolution of village settlements. Elsewhere in Britain this trend continued into the Iron Age with the evolution of towns based on large fortified camps or hill forts. In Scotland, however, this did not happen, or at least it did not happen in the Highlands and Islands. The reasons for this are many and complex but all relate to the increasing difficulty of winning a living from the land, the loss of the marginal lands to the encroaching peat and the contraction of the cultivable land into small widely separated pockets. There is a very real sense in which it can be argued that Scotland and Ireland (which was undergoing the same processes) were cut off from the mainstream of Western European civilisation at the end of the Late Bronze Age. Thereafter their status was elevated occasionally to that of distinctive cultures but never again to civilisation.

Ignorant of the fate which lay in store for it, Late Bronze Age Society was both vigorous and successful. All over the Highland Zone the remains of hut circles and field systems can be seen, often covering very large areas of land which is now marginal. Their absence from land now under cultivation has led some archaeologists to suggest that they deserted the richer heavier bottom lands for the hill slopes during this period. However, it is inconceivable that the best and most profitable lands would have been deserted, and indeed the

Bronze Age   10,000   9,000   8,000   7,000   6,000   5,000

remains of hut circles, represented only by those features which were dug into the soil, can be seen over much of Lowland Scotland, where they masquerade as 'ring groove houses'. In these instances the ring groove represents the remains of the lining wall, from which the bank has been removed and its remains spread by ploughing. The Western Isles and the Highland Zone in general are of the greatest importance for European archaeological studies of this period because they hold out the promise of surviving, complete Late Bronze Age landscapes preserved under the peat.

Bronze working and the knowledge of metallurgical techniques were introduced by the Beaker Folk. A brief initial 'copper age' seems to have taken place, especially in Ireland where copper ores were readily available. Mines of Bronze Age date are visible at Mount Gabriel in the south-west of Ireland (radiocarbon dated to the sixteenth century B.C.), and ores from this region played a large part in the development of the Bronze Age in the British Isles. Bronze is an alloy of copper and tin, ideally in the proportions of 90% copper to 10% tin. This ideal alloy is a eutectic alloy in that it has the lowest melting point of any alloy of these two metals, lower in fact than either of the parent metals. The advantages of this for the early metallurgist were so obvious that the 90/10 alloy rapidly became the norm. From the remains of early furnace sites it is possible to reconstruct the process of primitive smelting with some confidence. Smelting is the process of winning the metal from its ore, and this is partly achieved by the application of high temperatures but also by the chemical reaction known as reduction, which is achieved by the use of a bowl furnace. This was a clay-lined hemispherical hollow in the ground into which alternating layers of charcoal and ore were placed. This was ignited and covered with a second thick clay hemisphere. Air was draughted into the bowl furnace via a clay funnel called a tuyere, and exhaust gases were vented through a small hole at the top of the furnace. The smelted metal flowed down into the bottom of the bowl, making a plano-convex cake of copper. Fragments of furnaces, tuyeres and copper cakes all survive from a variety of sites. Similar simple furnaces were in common use for iron smelting in the Western Isles up into the eighteenth century.

>

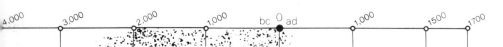

The earliest bronze objects were simple regular shapes which could be cast in open moulds. These were mainly solid axes and daggers. The earliest axes were shaped very like the polished stone axes of the Neolithic and were extremely wasteful of metal. In time the moulds became more sophisticated. The lost wax or *cire perdue* method was used for individual items. In this technique a wax model of the desired object was made first. This was then encased in fine clay with holes left for the entry and overflow of metal. The clay was then fired, the wax model melted and was thus 'lost' from the process. Finally the metal was poured in, and when cooled the clay was broken away to reveal the cast object. Last of all the bivalve moulds appeared. These were usually made of metal, in two main parts each of which had carved into it one face of the object to be cast. Projecting pins on one side which fitted into the holes on the other were used to line up the two halves of the mould. By the use of these techniques intricate and occasionally beautiful castings could be produced, most of them as sound as any produced in modern foundries.

The process of metallurgy does not end there, however. Bronze is highly ductile and can be hammered out into thin sheets or brought to find edges. Hammering also hardens the metal, and analyses of axes and swords often reveal that they have been hardened by hammering. This hardness is the result of the fracture of the crystalline structure of the metal and if pursued too far will make the metal brittle and cause it to crack and split. This can be offset by annealing or simply heating the metal and cooling it slowly. This relieves the crystalline deformations and allows further working. Again analyses of various objects have shown that the early smiths were familiar with this process.

Given the relative scarcity of the ores of copper and tin and the probably considerable distances over which they would have to be transported, it is unlikely that bronze was ever in common use or, indeed, readily available there. It is more likely that it was to a great extent a status metal possessed only by the upper levels of the evolving social hierarchy. Gold was also in use in the Bronze Age period, mainly for personal ornament, amongst which the lunulae are perhaps the most beautiful. Made of thin sheets of beaten gold and crescentic in shape, they are sometimes ornamented in the style and motifs of Beaker pottery.

The chronology of the Bronze Age is normally based on what are called typologies. These are developmental sequences of types of artefacts. Thus simpler examples of axes are believed to be earlier than more complex types, and so on. This archaeological version of stamp collecting is of varyingly questionable validity, especially in remote areas like the Western Isles were the old forms arrive late and persist long after they have been superseded elsewhere. On the basis of typologies the Bronze Age further south is divided into three periods, but the simple twofold division adopted here for the Highland Zone has a lot to recommend it.

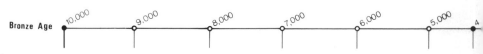

Bronze Age   10,000   9,000   8,000   7,000   6,000   5,000   4

An interesting phenomenon emerged during the typological 'late Bronze Age', and this was the adulteration of the metal with lead. In some cases, the effect on the strength of the resulting object would have been minimal, but in many it would have rendered them useless. Socketed axes seem in particular to have suffered in this way. Some archaeologists have speculated that this was the result of a period of infiltration when bronze which could be treated as currency because of its scarcity was devalued in this way.

Apart from personal ornaments and ornamented pottery and equipment, art seems to have arrived in the Western Isles in the Bronze Age. Relatively elaborate carvings are known from other areas from the preceding Neolithic period. The passage graves of the Boyne Valley in Ireland or the Breton Peninsula are well known for the proliferation of geometric patterns carved, on their kerb, passage and chamber stones. Such art, however, seems absent from sites in the Western Isles. During the Bronze Age a motif called the cup mark or cup and ring mark came to prominence. The cup mark is a simple hollow up to 0.1m in diameter and 0.03m or 0.04m deep carved into a stone. If a groove is carved, concentric with the cup mark, the resulting motif is the cup and ring mark. These have been found ornamenting the capstones or side stones of Bronze Age cists and on standing stones attributed to the Bronze Age. They occur in the Western Isles on outcrops of rock at six sites in North Uist, one of which, at Ard a Mhorain, is now covered at high tide. Other examples have been noted on Boreray and at Hacklett in South Uist and elsewhere. All of the known examples consist of cup marks alone, and the possibility that some of these are natural cannot be entirely discounted.

The end of the Bronze Age presents something of a mystery. Very few of the excavated sites in upland regions ranging, from Cornwall to Scotland have yielded radiocarbon dates later than, 1000 B.C. Pollen diagrams show, in general, a quite clear abandonment, of agriculture on the scale previously practised. This may be gleaned, to some extent, from the fact that on, the Isle of Arran, for example, the expansion of Late, Bronze Age society was such that the forest cover in the Machrie Moor area was wiped out within two centuries. Late, Bronze Age villages abound on the slopes around Machrie Moor, indicative of large stable populations. Where did they all go? Did some plague decimate them? Or was the steadily deteriorating environment finally incapable of supporting them in the numbers possible before the start of the first millennium B.C? Only further and intensive study will provide the answers to these questions, and it is clear that the Western Isles must be a key area for such studies. The concentration of stone circles around Loch Roag, for example, compares with the concentration of circles on Machrie Moor, and the absence of associated settlements in the Lewis area at the former must be accounted for by their burial beneath peat, because the pollen analyses from the area attest to their presence.

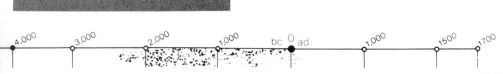

4,000   3,000   2,000   1,000   bc 0 ad   1,000   1500 1700

THE PEAT
CELTIC WARRIORS IN A DROWNING LANDSCAPE

The advent of iron working in southern and lowland Britain took place early in the first millennium B.C., possibly as early as 800 to 700 B.C.. But there is no reason to believe that the associated cultures or peoples became established in the Highlands and Islands for a further 500 years. Furthermore, evidence is now emerging which suggests that its inception in the upland zone of northern Britain coincided with a major collapse of the existing social and economic order. In general, the Later Bronze Age in the upland zone was a period of population increase, evidenced by an expansion of settlement up into what are now marginal lands. These settlements were village-like in their organisation: groups of circular houses often set in or beside apparent field systems in which clearance cairns are scattered. The ensuing Iron Age saw a reversion to single homesteads set in the midst of large territories with relatively little evidence for cultivation. Clearly there was more to the Iron Age than the mere introduction of a new metal.

However, the importance of the new metal would be hard to overstate. Unlike bronze, its ores were widely distributed and their reduction, by smelting, to metal a relatively simple process. It is clear from many excavations that virtually every Iron Age settlement produced its own metal, and iron ingots or fragments, slag from smelting and pieces of furnace linings and tuyeres are all relatively common finds. The ready availability of iron encouraged a great widening of the range of tools, weapons and other artefacts which were produced. Bronze continued in use also but was mainly employed in the production of personal ornaments, horse trappings, shield mounts and the like.

It is probably useful to point out here that as far as the Western Isles were concerned the Roman invasion might never have taken place. There are fewer than a handful of objects which can be identified as Roman from the quite numerous excavations of sites of Roman and later date in the islands. This lack of direct imput to the local tribes is not unique to the Isles. Native settlements, even south of the Antonine Wall, seem to have continued in existence with no direct evidence for Roman intrusion. North of the Wall it would be hard to deduce the presence of Roman invaders from the meagre quantities of identifiably Roman material which have been found. Only the large sites, like the lowland hill forts, seem by their contents and phases of use and abandonment to have been subject to Roman influence. Perhaps Roman society, based primarily on urban centres was indifferent to the largely rural settlement of the greater part of Scotland. In comparison we may note

Iron Age 10,000 9,000 8,000 7,000 6,000 5,000 4,000

This Iron **Age** midden site is undergoing excavation, on the coast at Hornish Point, South Uist.

that the influence of the British Raj on the ordinary Indian peasant was negligible, whilst that brought to bear upon the ruling heads of India's petty kingdoms, the Rajahs, destroyed their dominance, power and influence.

The Iron Age in the Isles, then, began late, possibly as late as 300 to 200 B.C., often in a period of population contraction and, once established, continued in existence, free from significant Roman interference, up to the Medieval period. In fact some of its basic

social and economic structures, including the clan system and runrig agriculture, continued in being, largely unaltered, into the eighteenth century. For our purposes, however, we shall consider that the Iron Age ran from 500 B.C. until about 600 A.D., at which time the introduction of Christianity created significant changes, exacerbated by the subsequent Viking invasions and settlement 200 years later.

During this period the climate in the Isles seems to have been largely similar to that which it currently enjoys — using the latter term in a loose sense. The start and end of the period were both somewhat wetter and colder than currently but, in general, the present constraints on cultivation, exposure to high winds and considerable wetness, were those faced by the Iron Age inhabitants. We have no direct evidence of fluctuation in sea levels at this time, but the current severe erosion of Iron Age sites in the Isles clearly indicates that the level was much lower than the level at present. That some, and in places severe, disruption of the coastal environment took place may be deduced from the observation of sites built on the shell sand machair which have suffered phases of burial, and erosion during their occupation. These sites, the coastal middens, are an important part of the Iron Age of the Western Isles.

N/E ViEW from CRAONAVAL (N.Uist)

Iron Age	10,000	9,000	8,000	7,000	6,000	5,000	4,000

The machair sands in which the middens lie are composed of crushed sea shells, mainly barnacle shells. Since these are made of calcium carbonate (or lime), the soils they form are completely opposite in their chemical characteristics, plant growth potential, drainage and other aspects to the heavy peat lands which make up the rest of the islands' land surfaces. The visitor will be struck by the obvious difference between the apparent richness of the machair grassland and the apparent poverty of the peat-covered hills, especially in South Uist where the long narrow shape of the island emphasises the difference. The islanders call the machair and peatlands the 'white' and 'black' lands respectively, and there is more to the naming than the simple observation of their respective colours. Nevertheless their extreme richness and poverty are largely apparent, and in practice both are relatively poor lands. Both can be cultivated, but only with difficulty, and both provide pasture which is relatively poor.

The problem with the machair is a somewhat technical one. Its high ph (its alkilinity) ties up trace elements in the soil which are vital to plants and animals alike. Also, it is a fragile soil because of its low humus content, and ploughing exposes it to erosion by the wind, leading at worst to loss of the sown crop. It is susceptible to drought in summertime and flooding, in places, in winter. However, the addition of humus, either as manure or as the more readily available peat or sea weed, overcomes almost all of these problems. Conversely, the addition of machair sand to the peat reduces its acidity and allows for cultivation. In areas too far from the sea the peat can be cultivated by 'muirburn'. This is the practice of ploughing or digging up the surface of an area of peat, allowing it to dry and then burning it. The ash deposited on the underlying peat reduces its acidity and allows the production of one or two crops of cereals such as barley. These artificial or manmade soils are called plaggen soils and, although productive, are very labour-intensive.

Examination of the coastal middens shows that they consist of three elements. Structures of various forms ranging from simple circular huts to complex wheelhouses occur on most sites, although they may not be very obvious since they will be cut in cross section by the sea, and cluttered with material from the eroding face and the beach. Round the structures deep deposits of refuse have accumulated, both household and farmyard. These can be up to 3m high and are rich in potsherds, animals bones, shell, slag, etc. Finally there are extensive areas of cultivated soils up to 1m thick which stretch away from the midden for distances of up to 300m to 400m. It is clear that these are plaggen soils since they contain recognisable peat and dung fragments. The coastal middens, then, were occupied by Iron Age peoples who were familar with the strengths and weaknesses of the machair and who found it possible to make the necessary, labour-intensive effort to cultivate it.

Rather more obvious than the midden sites are the stone-built forts, of various types, of Iron Age date which are scattered over the peat-covered parts of the islands. All types have strong defensive walls and are usually sited with a view to enhancing their defensibility. They commonly occupy the tops of low hills or are situated on small islands in lochs to which access is gained over causeways which are wholly or partly manmade. Their defensive nature can, however, be overemphasised since many of them cannot accommodate the numbers of warriors and their dependents necessary to effect an all-round defence of their circuits.

Iron Age

| 10,000 | 9,000 | 8,000 | 7,000 | 6,000 | 5,000 | 4,000 |

The brochs (pronounced brocks) are the largest and most impressive of the Iron Age structures, and the example at Dun Carloway in Lewis is second only to that at Mousa, Shetland in its size, complexity and state of preservation. Brochs occur only in Scotland and are restricted to the Western and Northern Isles and the north, particularly the north-east of mainland Scotland. The largest and most complete example, Mousa, is some 11m high and 8m internally, 16m in external diameter. Brochs are somewhat bottle-shaped in vertical section, the outer wall face taking a marked inturn like a modern cooling-tower. The inner face is vertical with one or more scarcements, or projecting courses of stone. Since few survive much higher than a single story, only one scarcement exists in the majority at a height of 2m to 3m above the old ground level. Recent excavations in Orkney suggest that brochs were in use in the period 300 B.C. to 300 A.D.

cavity WaLL .. o

The walls are drystone-built throughout, and their erection, without the use of mortar, must rank amongst the great engineering achievements of antiquity. They are hollow, that is to say they consist of an inner and outer face separated by galleries, the flag floors of which band the inner and outer faces together. Access to the galleries is usually by staircases, though at Mousa there is really only one gallery which rises in a helix, or extended spiral, from the lowest level to the wall top. The entrance is the only opening which pierces the composite wall. It is usually low and tunnel-like and strongly defensible. The entrance passage usually widens slightly, about a third to half way in, leaving two jambs against which the door or gate closed. Holes in the side walls housed a door bar which could be shot across immediately behind the door, securing it against the jambs. Pivot stones which served as the hinges on which the door turned are usually found behind the jambs.

Entrance — dùn carloway

Iron Age

10,000   9,000   8,000   7,000   6,000   5,000   4,000

In the Western Isles, the wall at ground level normally contains one or more chambers or galleries, unlike the broch walls of the Northern Isles which are normally solid. The intermural galleries, described above, begin at the first floor in both types. In Dun Carloway one of these cells opens onto the entrance passage and is considered to be a guard cell since anyone within it could hold the passage against enemies trying to force an entry. At Dun Carloway this cell can now only be entered from the eastern passage, but it also had a narrow creepway — now blocked — which connected it with the next cell and thence with the interior. The small size of the doorway is in part occasioned by the need to make it defensible, but it also reflects the difficulty in making safe openings through such enormously heavy walls. The load carried by the lintels of such openings is tremendous, and the broch builders evolved a way of lessening it. This was by making a series of openings one above the other, so that the lintels of the lowest did not have to carry the weight of the solid wall. This, of course, was only done in the interior wall since any openings to the outside presented an obvious weakness to any attacker, and these were kept to the absolute minimum so that the single entrance is the only break in the external wall. Weight-relieving apertures are visible at Dun Carloway rising above a first-floor-level door. This door probably gave access to a second story, with a wodden floor supported, in part, by the scarcement ledge, and by wooden posts erected in the broch's interior. Recent excavations in Orkney suggest that the broch interior was divided into radial segments with a clear central area in which a large stone-kerbed hearth was situated.

Dun Carloway and Dun Borve on Lewis are the best preserved of the Outer hebridean brochs and, together with Dun Cromore and Dun Loch an Duna, constitute the four known brochs on Lewis and Harris. A further four possible brochs, Duns Borve, Stuigh, Baravat, and Traigh na Beire, are recorded from Lewis and Harris. On North Uist only two, Dun Sticir and Dun Torcuill, are known, while Benbecula has none. For South Uist a further two, Dun Buidhe Ardnamonie and Dun na Buail Uachdraich, are recorded, with a third possible site at Dun Vulan. The differences which exist in every sphere, between the Outer and Inner Isles, are manifest also in the density of broch distribution. The total of fourteen sites for the Outer Isles, which includes all the possible broch sites, pales in comparison with Skye's twenty-eight; and even little Tiree has five.

Far more numerous, though smaller and less spectacular, are the duns, of which there are about 120 in the Outer Isles. Of these some twenty are known to have been used, or possibly reused, in the Medieval period. Duns are small fortified sites, usually roughly circular with a thick dry stone wall. Their distribution on the west coast of Scotland and in the islands overlaps that of the brochs. The walls are thick, commonly 3m or more, and the entrances are often fitted with door jambs and bar-holes like those of the brochs. In most cases the walls consist of a solid rubble core between built internal and external faces. Some, especially in the Outer Isles, contain chambers and galleries within the wall thickness and have stairways leading to the wall heads. In these details they closely parallel the brochs and some, known as 'semi brochs', seem to represent a transitional phase from duns to brochs. This has led some scholars to suggest that the duns of the Western Isles gave rise to the semi-brochs and ultimately the brochs which then spread north and eastwards, leading to the Mousa-type broch. However, there are now strong arguments against this theory. To begin with, the semi Broch of Dun Ardtreck has been radiocarbon dated to 55 b.c. ± 105 which makes it rather too late to be ancestral to the brochs. The excavation at Dun Cuier, Barra, a dun site, produced types of bone combs and moulds for glass beads which suggest a date

4,000   3,000   2,000   1,000   bc 0 ad   1,000   1500   1700

in the sixth or seventh century A.D. Thus, some of the duns are too recent to be ancestral to either brochs or semi-brochs.

The duns were single homesteads. In some cases they are small enough to have been roofed over, the rafters resting on the enclosing wall but, in general, excavation reveals that they contained one or more freestanding buildings and, possibly, lean-to sheds, built against the back of the wall. It is hard to believe that more than a single family could have occupied most duns, but some larger sites do exist where, perhaps, two or more family groups resided. Modern scientific excavation is desperately needed to help clarify almost every aspect of the lives of their inhabitants.

Rudhana Beighre   ☐ ☐   Clettraval

Promontory forts are also of Iron Age date, although the absence of excavation leaves us uncertain of their dating relative to the brochs and duns. However, a site near Barra Head lighthouse is of interest in that a galleried stone wall was built across the neck of the promontory to defend its landward side, 600 ft high cliffs providing adequately for this need on the seaward side. This site, now regrettably rather ruinous, is similar to the so-called 'block-houses' of the Orkneys and Shetlands whose parallels with broch construction include the entrance arrangements of jambs, barholes, etc. and stairways to the wall head as well as intermural galleries. The site of Ruadha na Beire near Barvas in Lewis may also have been of this type, but the wall there had been reduced to a meaningless jumble of stone.

Wheelhouses, the last drystone structures of Iron Age date in the Western Isles, have been aptly named. The circular structure is segmented internally by radial walls which leave a clear central area in which a hearth may be set. Thus, a series of bays is created around the inside of the wall, and these sometimes have a low kerb added to complete their division from the central area. These sites are commonly built into the slope of a hill or sand dune, or, as occurs at Clettraval, into the cairn of a Neolithic chambered tomb. Thus the whole or the greater part of the circuit of their wall is often only one stone thick, merely a facing to the sand or soil into which they have been cut. Sites which are cut into a slope in this way are often called earth houses, and

examples in the Isles include sites at the Udal, Foshigharry and Bac Mhic Connain, all in North Uist. These do not seem to differ from the free-standing examples like the site at Tigh Talamhanta, Allasdale or that at Usinish. A further sub-group, called aisled round houses, differs from the remainder only in that a gap exists between the radial piers and the house wall. Since this gap is only .75m to 1.25m wide, the term 'aisle' may seem a little grandiose.

Wheelhouse structures were inserted within the brochs at Clickhimmin in Orkney and Jarlshof, in Shetland, as secondary habitations and are thus apparently later than brochs in the Northern Isles. At the Udal, however, a radiocarbon date of 200 to 400 A.D. has been returned for the end of the wheelhouse occupation. In part, therefore, they overlap with the probable dating of the brochs.

Houses on crannogs, or manmade islands, are a feature of the Iron Age on mainland Scotland. The abundance of natural islands in the lakes of the Outer Isles probably eliminated the need for their construction there. One possible crannog is known, however, from Lewis. This is a structure of logs and stones and it lies in Loch Airidh na Lic, near Stornoway. Nothing is known of its actual date, form or construction; however, it need not even be of Iron Age date, since some crannogs were re-used in the Medieval period.

So much for the houses they lived in, what now of the residents of the Isles in the Iron Age? The Romans described the natives north of the Antonine Wall as *picti*, the Picts or 'painted ones'. The Picts are an almost complete mystery to us. We believe on no clear evidence that they were responsible for a large group of carved stones, of which one was found in the Western Isles. We believe that they were also responsible for a group of Ogham inscriptions which cannot be deciphered. In general we believe them to have been the pre-Celtic residents of Scotland who were gradually displaced from the Western Isles and Highland Scotland by the Irish (who were then called the Scoti!) and eventually amalgamated into the nation of Scotland under Kenneth MacAlpin in 841. When therefore we excavate anything which is later than the Bronze Age and earlier than the Scoti, the practice has been to call it Pictish. Thus little by little we have begun to create a people and a culture to fit the label of the Picts. The legitimacy of this process may be questioned. At any rate the Picts traded with Northern Irish Celts and were, probably from about the first or second centuries A.D., settled upon by the latter in the area of Kintyre and Argyll. Pictish artefacts are identified as such by their ornamentation or their dates and, in so far as may be judged from the archaeological record, they are not different from their Celtic counterparts. The duns of Atlantic Scotland find ready parallels, down to the smallest architectural detail, with Irish Celtic duns. If therefore the Picts did exist as something more than another tribe, clan or sept of Celts, their culture, reflected in the things they made or used, the houses they lived in and so on, was not significantly different from its Celtic counterparts. Thus, in describing Iron Age Scotland, we may rely on the evidence which exists for the Celts to provide for us a picture of that society and its economic and political organisation. If this does not precisely describe 'Pictland', it nevertheless describes a warrior aristocracy of a type common throughout Europe and surviving for a thousand years.

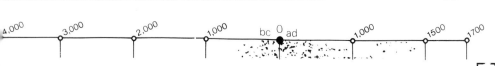

| 4,000 | 3,000 | 2,000 | 1,000 | bc 0 ad | 1,000 | 1500 | 1700 |

The Romans described Celtic society as consisting of a hierarchical organisation of kings, warriors, druids, plebs and slaves, in spirit, if not in detail. This view is borne out by the early Irish literature which survives to provide for us a window on the Iron Age: distorted and clouded perhaps, but nonetheless revealing a good deal of the social organisation of the Western Celts. Their society was rigidly hierarchical, a man's rights, duties and privileges being set by his rank, which in turn was determined by his birth. Some might improve their lot by outstanding valour in battle or by the triumph of their clan in battle but, for the majority, their lives were determined from the instant of birth. This type of society was a warrior aristocracy in which prestige and social power resided in the king and his warrior band. They were supported by free, and sometimes by enslaved, farmers, who provided for their overlord and his retinue in taxes of food and cattle. As families owed allegiance to their head who in turn was responsible for their conduct, so groups of families owed allegiance to the head of their kin group, who might call himself a king. Some 'kings' ruled kingdoms no bigger than parishes. Loose affiliations of kings in turn allied themselves to regional overlords, the 'clan chiefs' of later times, and so on, it almost seems *ad infinitum.*

Cattle formed the currency of the society, and in marginal areas such as the Highland Zone, cattle-raising gave rise to th Celtic cowboy. Dispersed settlements suited the ranching of cattle, each site placed near the centre of its territory. Cattle raiding was and is endemic to such societies, and so fortified settlements commonly emerge. The raiding allows for and requires the presence of warriors, and thus the social circle completes itself. The warriors ornament themselves, their horses, chariots and other equipment, and artisans emerge to provide these.

Against this brief outline of Iron Age society it is possible to offer a fuller interpretation of the buildings which we have described than simply that one succeeds the other in chronological order. Can it be that these are the residences of folk of different levels in that society? The wheelhouse, directly associated with the mechanics of farming, may be viewed as the house of a farmer, the dun as the residence of a middle-range chief or king, and the broch as the abode of a regional ruler. If this were so, the similarities in their architecture, in their dating, in the artefacts they contain and in their internal organisation would all be explained. By their internal organisation we mean their common tendency to be radially segmented. The bays thus produced may be the 'imdae' to which frequent reference is made in the early literature. Dr. Hilary Murray has studied these references and believes that the imdae were compartments or areas divided off within the house. Some were apparently personal spaces, some bed spaces, and some may have served special functions, like storage or working areas. Certainly the radial compartments would meet these needs.

There is a tendency nowadays, especially among the Edinburgh middle classes and the readers of 2000 A.D., to romanticise the Celts, and Iron Age folk in general. No doubt there were those for whom life was all love, beer and cattle raiding, but one suspects that for the majority it may have tended rather to the short, nasty and brutish side of things. The most impressive thing about the Iron Age settlement of the Outer Isles is not the majestic brochs, nor yet the lonely duns, but rather the way in which the food producers, the farmers and herdsmen exploited the already impoverished landscape. Their efforts supported a society which was clearly a vital one and, in comparison, much of what followed was an anticlimax. ●

Iron Age

LIGHT AND DARK
THE ARRIVAL of CHRISTIANITY AND THE COMING of THE VIKINGS

The first five centuries A.D. saw in Ireland the emergence and the rise to ascendancy of the Ui Neill family. They originated in the Southern Midlands of Ireland, and their increase in power kept pace with their gradual movement northwards, pressing into the traditional homelands of the Ceneil Connell, one sect of which, the Dal Riata or Dalriada, were ultimately forced out of north-east Ireland into Kintyre and Argyll. By about 500 A.D. these people were sufficiently numerous and well established to transfer their capital from Ireland to Scotland. The Irish intruders were known as the Scoti (which meant 'Irish' at that time!), and the people whose lands they usurped were the enigmatic Picti, or the Picts.

Armorial slab at the site of **Howmore**, South Uist.

▷▷

Early
Christian

10,000   9,000   8,000   7,000   6,000   5,000   4

During the latter part of this period Christianity arrived in Scotland in a series of separate and not always successful waves. Some of the Roman silverware discovered at the important hillfort of Traprain Law in East Lothian, near Edinburgh, bear the Chi-Rho monogram, and a silver flagon is decorated with biblical scenes. These attest the presence of Christianity in Late Roman Scotland (early fifth century A.D.). About the same time Saint Ninian is described by Bede as the bishop of a see based at Whithorn, Wigtownshire in the south-west of Scotland. The people resident between Hadrian's Wall and the Antonine Wall at that time were the tribes of the Britons, who spoke a variety of Celtic, known as P-Celtic, akin to the Welsh or Breton languages.

North of the Antonine Wall lived the Picts, who are believed to have spoken a non-Celtic, indeed a non-Indo-European and thus wholly archaic language, and on the west coast of Scotland the Scots, who like the Irish spoke Q-Celtic. It was via the latter that Christianity was introduced into Northern Scotland, notably by Saint Columba of Iona. Columba arrived on the island of Iona in 563 A.D. and, although Iona lay within Dalriada, his use of the island was apparently sanctioned by the Pictish king, Bridei, whose court was situated near Inverness. It seems that at least occasionally the Scots were under Pictish overlordship.

Celtic Christianity of the type introduced by Columba was based on the monastic ideal and centred on monasteries under the control of abbots. This contrasts with the contemporaneous Roman-based Christianity which was organised in dioceses and parishes under the control of bishops. In a Celtic monastery the bishop was subservient to the abbot. A typical Celtic monastery consisted of a cashel, an area enclosed by a wall or a ditch and bank, within which were sited churches, chapels, or oratories together with accommodation for the clerics. Very few true cashels are known in Scotland, Iona being a notable exception. The site of Teampull Chaluim Cille in Benbecula seems to have consisted of a cashel with its church located some small distance away. At Howmor in South Uist two churches and two of an original three chapels survive, and at Kilbar on Barra a single church is accompanied by two chapels. The doorways of these churches are trabeate, i.e. have inclined door jambs so that the doorway narrows toward the top. Trabeate doorways are characteristic of Celtic churches and oratories (see information box). These groups of sites may represent cashels the enclosing elements of which have been removed or buried.

▲ This modern cross has been erected within one of the chapels
The east wall of the church called An Teampull More, at Howmore South Uist ▼

Early
Christian

10,000   9,000   8,000   7,000   6,000   5,000

The importance of the wall or bank enclosing such early monuments cannot be over-emphasised. The area thus enclosed was the area of sanctuary within which the law of the land did not run. It was subject only to church law, and fugitives from local justice could take refuge there with a certain degree of impunity. However, sanctuary was not always respected, and the early annals abound in records of those slain 'in the doorway of the church'. A more important, though less dramatic, role of the area enclosed and protected by God's — ecclesiastical — law was its use as a repository of the temporal wealth of the surrounding area. Iron Age communities seem in general to have followed the unendearing practice of constantly raiding their neighbours, mainly for cattle, but presumably for such other portable wealth as could be garnished. The role of the church in providing storage and shelter, ostensibly inviolable, against such raids may well have laid the basis for the Viking raids which were to come.

The difficulty noted above, of identifying cashel enclosures on Scottish, Early Christian sites, is second only to the difficulty of identifying many of the sites themselves! For many such sites only the evidence of local placenames indicates the probable existence of monastic settlement or churches of the early period. The oldest placename element appears to be *annait* (or *Annaid*), and this is peculiar to the Early Christian Church. It is translated as meaning the mother church or founding community in the earliest Christian settlement of the area. On the Isle of Skye the enclosure called Annait, near Dunvegan Castle, contains the remains of a church and two hut circles amongst a range of probably later buildings. However, only the name survives on the Shiant Isles and at Shador, on Lewis, where it occurs in the plural form, *na hAnnaidean*.

The word 'Cill' usually rendered as 'Kill...' is a common placename element in the Western Isles. It derives ultimately from the Latin *Cella*, or church, and like Teampull — derived from the Latin *Templum*, or temple, is usually followed by a saint's name, thus Kilpatrick or Teampull Eoin. Where either term is followed by a Celtic name, the site may be attributed to the Celtic church. However, placename evidence is not without its difficulties and ambiguities. To begin with the 'Kil' prefix may derive from words other than Cill meaning 'church'. It may derive from *Coille* a wood or *coal* a strait — as in Kilbrannan Sound between Arran and Kintyre. Also, whilst the addition of a saint's name, during the Early Christian Period, implies some sort of proprietorial right of the founder of the original foundation, it became the practice, in the Medieval period, to dedicate every church to some saint. Thus, of the many churches named after Saint Columba in the Western Isles, a majority may represent dedications in his honour dating to the Medieval period, especially as the saint himself is not recorded as having visited the Western Isles.

The dedications to Saint Barr or Finbarr, the founding saint of Cork, in the Irish Republic, which are found in the Western Isles may also relate to the cult of that saint's worship which grew up in the Medieval period, probably in Northern Ireland. Thus Cille Bharra or Kilbar on the Isle of Barra, though clearly existing at an earlier date, may owe its dedication to the revived interest in Saint Finbarr in the twelfth century.

At the opposite end of the Long Island the dedication of the church at Eoropie, in Ness, near the northern tip of Lewis is not without its interest. This architecturally anomalous churh is dedicated to Molua — *Teampull Maluadh*. The 'mo' part of this name is an honorific prefix, a respectful mode of address, whilst the Lua is believed to be the Celtic and pagan god Luaidh. This Christianisation of a pagan god is not exceptional, indeed, the character of Brigid, the foremost female Celtic saint, subsumes attributes which are clearly pre-Christian in their origin. One may even wonder at the Christianity of Columba's first act on coming to Iona: the burial alive of Odhran. His body was dug up again three days later and found to be very much alive. Odhran stood up in the grave and proclaimed that there was no hell, at which point he was slain for his heresy and reburied!

However difficult the location of the early churches may now prove and however doubtful their associations with the saints after whom they are named, there is no doubt that the advent of Christianity had a considerable impact on the Western Isles and the Highlands as a whole. The pollen record from Iona, for example, shows that the arrival of the Early Christians is coincident with a huge upsurge in cultivation, particularly in arable cultivation, on the island. The overall impression is one of a virtually uninhabited island being suddenly populated and brought into profitable cultivation. In point of fact we know from Adamnan's life of Saint Columba that the island was not uninhabited, and so we can be sure that the change in the island's status is directly due to the activities of the newly arrived missionaries.

The success of the early monastic settlements was by no means confined to Iona. They seem, in general, to have been hugely successful both in spiritual and temporal matters. Without disregarding the purely spiritual content of their message, it can be suggested that the Early Christians had at least two major features working in their favour. The first of these was that they provided a new social factor in a society which was far more rigidly organised and regimented than any we could imagine. Thus, a commoner could become an abbot and the equal of princes. Of course the great families rapidly moved to gain advantage in this and sent their sons to the church for reasons which may not always have been altruistic. Columba himself was a prince of the Ui Neill and had a claim, albeit not a very direct one, on the kingship of that tribe. A mere eleven years after his arrival we find him, and through him the church, in the role of 'kingmaker' with the inauguration at Iona of Aedan, in 574 A.D. This role is hardly compatible with that of the ascetic, hermetic life style so often claimed for the early churchmen.

Recent excavations at Iona give us a clue to the second factor in their success in that evidence was discovered suggesting that the Early Christian Church was able to introduce agricultural technologies suited to the cultivation of the heavy, peaty, wet soils which dominated the Highlands at the time. Undoubtedly access to classical sources and to the information to be gleaned from traders would have been factors in the provision of the necessary

Early
Christian

| 10,000 | 9,000 | 8,000 | 7,000 | 6,000 | 5,000 | 4 |

information. This, coupled with the availability of a centrally organised, well disciplined labour fource which, in the persons of the clerics themselves, was 'non profit making', provided a secure basis for the growth of prosperity and wealth.

The wealth of the major monasteries led within a century to their patronage of the arts on a scale which gave rise to the 'golden age' of the seventh and eighth centuries. The illumination of manuscripts, manufacture of metal objects and sculpting of stone crosses were undertaken to serve liturgical needs but were organised and financed on a scale which allowed their production as works of art. The association of nearby Iona with the Book of Kells and the preservation there of elaborate high crosses show that such artistic achievement was not absent from Scotland's western seaboard. However, the existence and predominance of Iona seems to have precluded the emergence of a strong, monastic centre in the Western Isles. Indeed there are very few sculptures of the Early Christian period in the Western Isles, and those which survive are very simple monuments.

:) modern burial area at Howmore (:

Slabs bearing simple Latin crosses, probably used as grave markers, are to be found at Clach an Teampull, Taransay; Teampull Mhuir, Vallay, North Uist; and Bagh ban, Pabbay. A slab of this type was removed from a building near St Taran's church, Taransay to the National Museum of Antiquities in Edinburgh. In general such slabs probably date to the seventh century or earlier, but it must be remembered that these are very simple structures and could also be of much later date. The Western Isles also contain a group of rude (or rough) stone crosses often with short, wide arms pierced by holes in the four angles between the arms and the shaft of the cross. Examples are visible at Cill Mhoire, Haugary, North Uist; Cille Pheadair, near Balelone, North Uist; and at Teampull Mhuir, Vallay. The dates of these monuments are even harder to determine than that of the cross-inscribed slabs. In general, however, it is probable that they are earlier than the eighth century in date. The island of North Rona preserves a small group of rude stone crosses beside the very simple and clearly very early church and may indicate a generally early — i.e. sixth or seventh century — date for such crosses.

A simple slab from Bagh Ban, Pabbay bears witness to the christianising of the Picts. The slab bears two Pictish symbols, the 'crescent', with V-rods and the 'flower' which are surmounted by a simple incised cross-potent (that is to say a cross the ends of whose arms and or shaft are crossed with short lines). The slab is now in the National Museum of Antiquities in Edinburgh in company with the second — and only other — Pictish carving from the Isles, that from Strome Shunnamul, Benbecula.

6

Pictish Symbol STONE

Early Christian

10,000   9,000   8,000   7,000   6,000   5,000   4,0

Even in the absence of well-preserved Early Christian churches in the Western Isles it is possible to suggest the forms of the churches themselves by inference from the types then current in Ireland and elsewhere in Scotland. Drystone-built, beehive-shaped structures, called 'clochain' (plural) or 'clochan' (singular), seem to have been used at first. Examples abound on the south-west coast of Ireland and are to be seen on the Island of Eileach an Naoimh in the Garvellochs and elsewhere in Scotland. For these, it is suggested, a church, rectangular in plan and shaped rather like an upturned boat, was developed. The doorways to both of these structures narrowed with height and usually carried a massive lintel. This seems to have been the origin of the trabeate doorway, and it is a characteristic feature of Celtic churches. The boat-shaped oratories were replaced in time by simple rectangular churches with massive vertical walls supporting a stone roof. The roofs were very steeply pitched so that their great weight would not push the tops of the supporting walls outwards, collapsing the structure. As the churches grew in size, voids and supporting arches were built into the roofs to reduce the weight and help carry it vertically onto the supporting walls. This, then is the developmental sequence of the Irish stone roof series first described by Harold Leask.

Apart from the anomalous sites on the Pygmy Isles, no complete clochan survives in the Western Isles. The chancel of the church in North Rona, however, is a fine, if rather fragmentary, example of a boat-shaped oratory. As commonly occurs, this early oratory was used as a chancel when the church was expanded by the addition of a simple rectangular nave. No complete stone-roofed church survives in the Isles, but thick-walled ruins with trabeate doors do occur.

7

8

Cross SLAB of Manx - type ⌄

THe Vikings

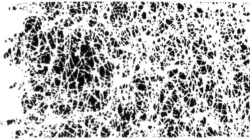

The Vikings constitute one of the major
mysteries of the archaeology of the
Western Isles in that while they occupied
and ruled the islands for almost 500
years, there are virtually no monuments
which can confidently be attributed to
them. They knew the Western Isles as
the 'Sudreyar' or 'Southern Isles',
Orkney and Shetland being the
'Nordreyar' or 'Northern Isles'. Their
ownership of the Western Isles was
recognised by the rest of Celtic Scotland
which named the isles 'Innsegall', the
'isles of the foreigners'. The extent of
the Viking domination may also be
gauged from the fact that 99 of the 126
recognisable village names on Lewis are
of wholly Scandinavian origin, while a
further 11 are partly Scandinavian in
origin. Thus, almost 99% of these
placenames must be attributed to the
Vikings. There can therefore be little
doubt that the Viking settlement of the
Western Isles was very extensive indeed.
It has even been suggested that the Isles
became overpopulated in the ninth
century and that some Viking settlers
moved away; some to Iceland where
their presence is recorded in written
documents, and some to the Faroes,
England and Normandy, where place-
and personal names reveal their
presence. The absence of Viking
settlement is therefore a real mystery.

Early
Christian

10,000 9,000 8,000 7,000 6,000 5,000 4,0

From the eleventh century the Sudreyar, together with the Isle of Man, formed the Kingdom of Man and the Isles. This was ruled — ultimately — by the King of Norway. After the middle of the twelfth century, when Somerled acGillibride had emerged as the chieftain of Argyll, the Isles were severed from Man. Following Somerled's invasion of Man of 1156, he forced the surrender of the Isles south of Ardnamurchan Point to himself, whilst those to the north remained subject to Norway. The Norwegian connection weakened with time but continued in being until the Battle of Largs, in 1263, saw the incorporation of the Isles into the Scottish Kingdom, following the defeat of the Norse under King Haakon.

The mystery surrounding the Vikings does not end with the absence of obvious relics of their presence. What became of the inhabitants whom they, presumably, replaced? The sagas, notably Egil's Saga, imply or, as in the latter case, state that the Norwegian Vikings settled in deserted places, amongst which the Hebrides are named. That there were at least some inhabitants cannot, however, be doubted, regardless of the saga's claim. The Vikings named several areas for the hermits who lived in them and whom they called 'papar'. Thus at least the four islands called 'Pappay' in the Outer Isles were occupied at the time. There is no good reason for supposing that the Iron Age/Early Christian population was either gone or exterminated, and there are good indications that neither had occurred. The units in which land is held tells us a lot about those who hold it, and in the Sudreyar the Vikings held the land in the pre-existing, essentially Celtic units: unlike the situation in the Nordreyar where the land was redivided on the Viking pattern of 'penny-lands' and 'ouncelands'. Further, the Vikings were relatively quickly converted to Christianity — at least in part — an event which would, no doubt, have been facilitated by the presence of a Christian community. One interesting example of this process is evidenced in the rune-inscribed cross slab from the church at Cille Barr on Barra (now in the National Museum of Antiquities in Edinburgh). It bears the inscription 'eptir Thorgered u Steinars dottur es kross sja reista', 'after Thorgerd, Steinar's daughter is this cross erected'. The runes are on the reverse of the slab, the face of which bears a cross of a type characteristic of the Isle of Man. The Norwegian scholar, professor Aslak Liestol, has suggested a possible explanation for the presence of this 'Manx' cross in the Sudreyar, in that Bjorn, the father of Gautr who claimed to have made all the crosses in Man, was born on the nearby Isle of Coll. This may imply that all the Manx crosses are ultimately derived from this prototype.

Given the abundant but indirect evidence for Viking settlement in the Sudreyar, why is it that we cannot find their houses? The typical Viking house was a long rectangular building divided along its length into three parallel strips. The two outer strips were slightly raised, and the beds were located there. The centre strip contained the hearth, and the normal domestic activities seem to have been concentrated in this strip, especially in the area of the hearth. Once abandoned, these houses rapidly decay to leave simple rectangular mounds in which, at best, only the outline of the outer wall remains visible. In this state they are not really distinguishable from the very numerous remains of blackhouses (see Chapter 8 for details) deserted or abandoned within the last two centuries. The solution to the problem of the absence of Viking settlement may therefore be that we simply are not seeing them in the midst of the abundant remains of similar, but much later, structures.

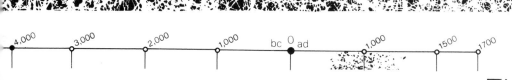

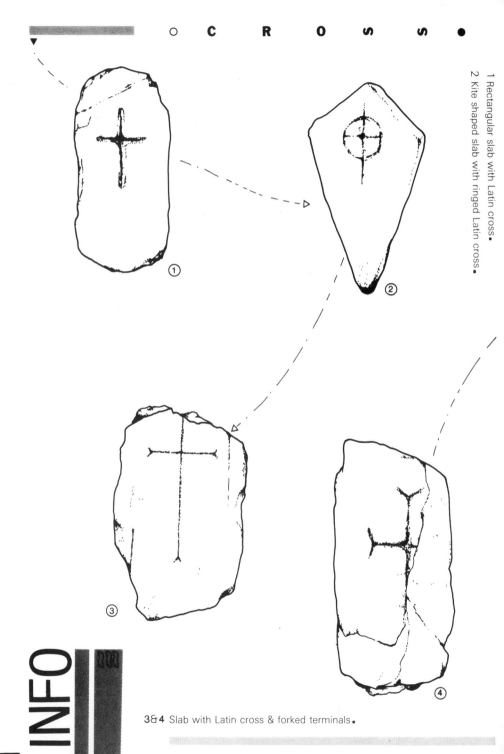

1 Rectangular slab with Latin cross ▪

2 Kite shaped slab with ringed Latin cross ▪

3 & 4 Slab with Latin cross & forked terminals ▪

INFO

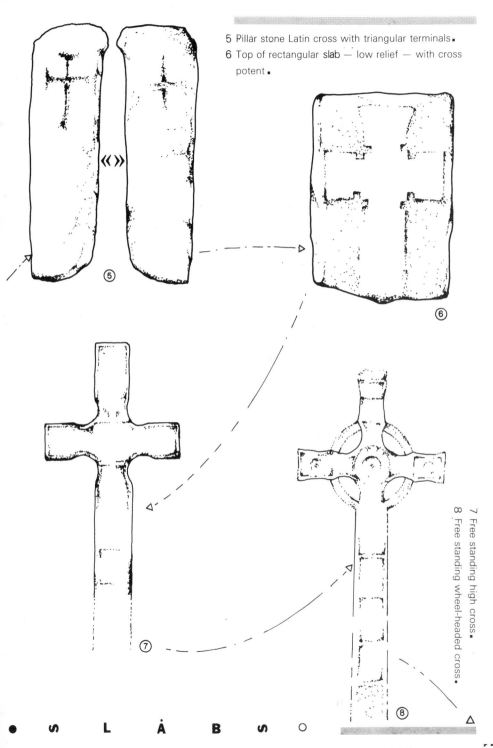

5 Pillar stone Latin cross with triangular terminals.
6 Top of rectangular slab — low relief — with cross potent.

7 Free standing high cross.
8 Free standing wheel-headed cross.

● ᔕ L Å B ᔕ ○

ECHOES of THE LORDSHIP of THE ISLES
ASPECTS of POST-MEDIEVAL SETTLEMENTS DEDUCED FROM SEVENTEENTH CENTURY RECORDS

7»

CHAPTER

After the defeat of the Norse in the mid-thirteenth century the Sudreyar reverted to the Scottish Crown, and the period which followed saw the emergence of the powerful lords who controlled the Isles and the west coast with a considerable degree of autonomy. In fact the origins of the Lordship could with reason be extended back to Somerled Mac-Gillebride's seizure of the southern part of the Isles a century earlier.

The swift assertion or reassertion of the Celtic nature of the Isles and the adjacent mainland poses a question: to what extent had they been absorbed into the Viking world? On the face of it, the completeness of the process of 'Celticisation' suggests that the pre-Viking Celtic settlers of the area had neither been exterminated nor wholly absorbed by their Norse overlords. By the time documentary evidence begins to provide useful insights — the early seventeenth century — that Celtic system was already beginning to break down, and a century later the bond between clan chief and clansman, the cornerstone of the Celtic system, was so weakened that the clansmen were cleared from the land for the economic advantage of their chiefs.

We know very, very little indeed of the social, political or economic life of the Isles from the beginning of the Lordship until the seventeenth century. Not only are documents lacking but buildings of the period, the castles, towers, churches and manors of lowland Scotland and

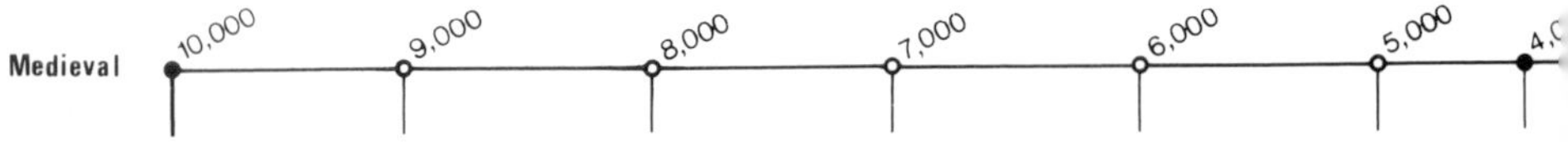

Medieval   10,000   9,000   8,000   7,000   6,000   5,000   4,0

England, simply do not exist in the Isles, or at least have not been identified there. Amongst the reasons for this the small population must be one of great importance. The late Lord Cooper of Culross estimated that Scotland's population in 1300 was about 400,000 souls, of whom only 50,000 were resident in the entire Highlands and Islands. It is now argued that his estimate may be low, but no one has seriously questioned the proposition of one eighth of the population which he attributed to that enormous area. Also, the holdings in the Western Isles were very large and were held by a very few lairds, some of whom, like MacDonald of Sleat, owner of North Uist, were non-resident in the Outer Isles. Thus the scarcity there of great houses need not be wondered at unduly. Given the lack of contemporaneous written record and the absence or unidentifiability of sites of the period, how may we learn anything of it? One way is to consider the state of affairs in the seventeenth century and from that to try to extrapolate backwards in time those features which seem to be traditional or established practices.

One effect of the alignment of the Lords and major landholders of the Outer Isles with the Scottish Crown was the confirmation of landholdings and the fixing of the main clan lineages. The clan chiefs were no longer dependent on the vote of their clansmen, and the earlier bewildering gains and losses of lands in interclan and internecine warfare were largely halted. MacDonald of Sleat's ownership of North Uist (not in fact completed until 1628) has already been noted. Barra was owned by the MacNeills, Harris and Glenleg on the mainland were owned by Macleod of Dunvegan, and Lewis by the Mackenzies of Seaforth. The Captain of Clanranald owned the greater part of South Uist, Begistill in the south-west being owned by MacNeill of Barra. Thus the greater part of the Long Island was owned by a mere handful of men, whose power in their own lands was virtually absolute. Externally they were overshadowed by the clans which held extensive west-coast estates, amongst whom were the Earls of Seaforth, owners of Lewis. The lords of Argyll, however, were the dominant influence in the western area as a whole. The MacLeans of Duart lost their island estates as a result of their accumulated debts, but in fact the prime cause of their loss was the inimical influence of Argyll.

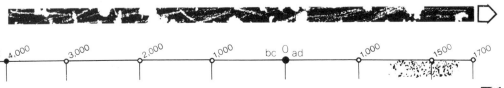

4,000   3,000   2,000   1,000   bc 0 ad   1,000   1500   1700

Clearly these great landowners did not work their lands directly. Rather the lands were rented out in a variety of ways to a variety of people. Lands were held by the vassals (or tenants) from a superior who could, himself, be a vassal to a higher superior. In general lands were leased or rented for fixed periods and, on the death of a vassal before their expiry, they could be inherited by his heir, male or female. It is fortunate, indeed, that amongst the documents of seventeenth-century date are several that describe an early system of land tenure in which echoes of a purely Celtic origin can be discerned. This was known as ward holding and was based on payment by the tenant to the landowner of military service and of lump-sum cash payments, called 'casualties'. The main casualty was 'wardship' which arose where the inheritor of a tenancy was a minor; in this event all revenues from the estate were payable to the landlord, until the inheritor achieved majority. 'Relief' was the casualty payable when a new tenant became the vassal of a landowner. The landlord retained the right to find a marriage partner for the heir of a tenancy, if the heir was a minor. Even in the early seventeenth century these casualties were being replaced by cash payments. Later the entire system gave way to that of feu farm, a simple and more truly feudal arrangement whereby the vassal paid a fixed annual rent for the duration of the lease. This annual rent was called feu duty, and was usually set as a sum of money, although it was commonly paid in kind, i.e. by the barter of goods in lieu of coinage. Services could still be specified as essential components of the feu duty, however, and certain services became almost standard.

The Captain of Clanranald obtained a crown charter in 1610 in respect of Crown lands held by him in South Uist. The feu duty consisted, in this instance, of an annual rent of £46 and the upkeep of a house and grounds and the provision of personal service including military service, for his superior. The provision of 'hosting and hunting' was a common feature of leases in the Isles. Hosting was the organisation of people for military service and their transport to, and leadership in, military campaigns.

Since the provision of services remained a feature of feu farm leases, the major difference between these and wardholding lay in the fact that the former provided a regular source of income to the landowner. This was clearly to be preferred to the admittedly much larger sums paid intermittently under the system of wardholding. After losing their autonomy, the Lords of the Isles increasingly turned to the east and south and sought the company and the ways of lowland lairds. This called for hard cash, a commodity of relatively little importance during the earlier period of the Lordship of the Isles. Thus social pressure was added to the trend towards the commercialisation of land tenure in the Isles.

The tenants who held land in the Outer Isles are readily divisible into groups. On the one hand some held large areas of land consisting of several townships; on the other, the small tenant might only hold a very small fraction of the land of a single township. Some of the larger tenants held a written lease, from the landowner, which was called a 'tack', and such men were called 'tacksmen'. In later periods the term seems to have been used to describe both tenants and agents of the landlords or, indeed, agents of the larger tenants. The Privy Council regulations of 1616, in limiting the number of retainers a chief could maintain in his company, encouraged the development of tenantry. They also specifically enjoined the chiefs to let their lands to tenants for fixed and clear duties. Thus the chief who of old kept

Medieval 10,000 9,000 8,000 7,000 6,000 5,000 4,00

his gentlemen about him, ever ready for raid or defence, could now convert his responsibility for their support to a formal lease of lands which would sustain them. It is hard to escape the conclusion that prior to the 1616 regulations the extent of settlement and the amount of land in profitable use must have been significantly less than in the period which followed.

Even among the 'gentlemen' the extent of the lands held varied considerably, and while most were held in multiples of townlands, some few were as little as half of a townland. Similarly, the duration of the lease was extremely variable. Many, if not most, were for a certain number of generations and/or a number of years. In South Uist, for example, five tacks were issued by John MacRonald, in 1625–6, each for two lifetimes and eleven years. Some, however, were for much shorter periods, but most of the very short leases, those of five years or less, were restricted to the Inner Hebrides and the small isles of the Argyllshire coast. It is probably true to say that the longer tacks of the Outer Isles are indicative of the survival there to a greater degree than elsewhere of the old clan loyalties.

Some of the services of the 'gentlemen of the chief's entourage' of earlier times carried over to be borne by the tacksman. Common amongst these was the provision of facilities for hunting: mainly deer hunting, but hawking is also specifically mentioned. The collection of monies due to the chief, and the porterage of payments in kind for him also fell to the tacksman's lot. It seems clear that many tacksmen of the seventeenth century were the immediate relatives of the clan chief. A century later, of course, the old loyalties began to wane, and outsiders brought in, often at high cost, who treated their subtenants abominably to produce the

▷

4,000　　3,000　　2,000　　1,000　　bc　0　ad　　1,000　　1500　1700

cash which they needed to recover their investments, make a profit and provide cash for the landowning chiefs. Thence to the clearances was but a short step.

The vast majority of tenants were not tacksmen: they were effectively peasants holding small parts of a townland either directly from the landowners or from a tacksman. Sometimes a townland was let to a group of tenants, called 'joint tenants', who held it directly from the landowner, without intervening tacksmen. Somewhere between a third and a half of the land was in the possession of joint tenants. The number who shared a townland ranged from two or three up to twenty or more, and their individual payments could also vary considerably, presumably in proportion to the amount of land or other resources they held. In Lewis, in the early eighteenth century, there were twenty tenants in Barvas and thirty-nine in Shawbost. Rents were extracted, partly in cash, £50 being a typical rent for a whole township, and partly in kind. The latter was calculated, per pennyland, at four stone of victual, four quarts of butter, four stone of cheese and four wethers per annum. The leases of small tenants were often issued annually, and Martin Martin, describing the Isles in 1695, or thereabouts, noted that the, unwritten, lease was granted by the proprieter giving a stick and some straw to the tenant who immediately returned it, thereby sealing the bargain.

The major products of the Isles throughout this period, and probably since the Iron Age, were barley, of the type called bere (also 'bear'), oats, dairy products, cattle and sheep.

The farming township consisted of a number of blackhouses, typically ten or twelve of them, sometimes called the 'winter Towns', set in close by the arable land. These were known as Bailtean (singular Baile), except for those which boasted churches, the 'kirktowns' of lowland Scotland which, in the west, were called 'clachans'. The baron courts, which were empowered to regulate agriculture on the west coast and to arbitrate agricultural disputes, introduced several acts requiring the construction of head dykes and march dykes by each baile. The head dyke was a bank, usually of earth or peat, constructed around the arable and 'in field' pasture and intended to keep out the animals while crops grew and ripened in the unfenced fields. The march dykes were similarly constructed and divided the common land of each township from that of its neighbours. With that glorious disregard for silly regulations which still inspires them, the Hebrideans ignored these regulations in the main. The arable and infields were abandoned each summer to the care of the young and very old, and the township's population moved out, and usually up, to the summer pastures on the moorland. Here they occupied flimsy buildings called 'shielings', the ruins of which are scattered all over the Isles, often encumbering archaeological sites. The herds were tended by herdsmen, making the building of dykes a relatively futile and unnecessary task. Presumably peat cutting was undertaken during the summer months to provide the winter fuel. The sheds, vans and assorted — occasionally surreal — shelters which are now visible in areas of peat cuttings are presumably survivals of earlier shielings. To see a bog scattered over with groups of folk cutting and stacking peat of a summer's evening is a fine sight and one redolent of the islands' past.

In theory and — here one must remember the islanders' high regard for theories! — the infields were cultivated in a cycle of crop and fallow seasons. They received such manures as were to be had, mainly seaweed and some animal drug. They were expected to produce the staple crops, oats and barley with some rye, both for the payment of rent, and also in the days before the widespread cultivation of the potato, to feed the tenants and their families. In general the level of husbandry was low. It is suggested that cereal yields of 2 or 3 for 1 (measures yielded for measures planted) were the norm. The practice of harvesting the crop by uprooting the plants may have speeded the harvest and provided straw for thatch and animal bedding, but it certainly impoverished the land. Attempts to improve things by introducing peas as a potential crop, a decree issued by the baron courts, seems to have either failed or been ignored. Nonetheless it must be assumed that sufficient was produced to keep body and soul together and to meet the rent. It is not clear to what extent fishing supplemented the diet of the farmer, but this abundant supply of protein must surely have been exploited. Several attempts were made through the course of the seventeenth century to establish fishing on a commercial basis. Dutch fishermen were brought to Lewis to found a fishing industry and to disseminate their skills, but the industry seems to have failed and the Dutchmen returned home.

The relative poverty and lack of success in arable farming were not matched in animal husbandry. Horses, cattle, sheep, pigs and goats were all kept, in varying quantities. A small farmer would usually have one horse, and larger farmers more, but the availability of hill pasture and winter feed, or rather their lack, militated against the maintenance of more. Sheep were kept universally, and even the poorest cottar kept two or three for wool, mutton and milk. Like the horses, the sheep were wintered out, often having to eat seaweeds when the hill pastures were grazed bare. The cattle, on the other hand, were treated with far more care, partly because they simply could not ▷

▷ survive the winter without adequate feeding, but mainly because of their economic importance. The cattle supplied dairy products, meat and hides and, beyond that, could be used to pay debts or could be sold off for cash. They represented a form of mobile wealth which could be taken to the distant markets of Lowland Scotland and England and converted to cash. The Isles produced almost nothing else that could generate hard currency, and certainly nothing that could generate it on the same scale. The cattle trade from the Isles is undoutedly ancient, probably rooted in the Iron Age traditions of the 'Celtic cowboys'. By the seventeenth century, however, it was organised on a large scale. Transactions valued at £2,000 were taking place in the 1630s, such as that between Campbell of Cawdor and a Glasgow merchant for the supply of 183 head of cattle. By the end of the century landlords, tacksmen and tenants in the Western Isles were all involved, in some way, in the trade. In general the tenant paid some or all of the rent in cattle, as did the tacksman. Then the proprietor hired a drover and paid his expenses, being repaid only after the cattle were sold. The drover bore the cost of losses incurred en route. Sometimes the landlord organised the drover himself, and occasionally tenants supplied cattle to independent drovers who organised what became known as public droves. To do the latter was at times a risk since some of the independent drovers did not have the capital to pay the farmers if the herd was lost to disease or theft on route to market.

The development of the cattle trade kept pace with the landlords' increasing need for cash. Part of this need arose out of the import of large — indeed very large — amounts of wines and spirits. The Statutes of Iona of 1609 tried to limit this legendary consumption and proclaimed that the import of liquor was prohibited, except to 'gentlemen', and then only for the use of their own households. Nonetheless the import continued, often in shiploads. The purchase of fine cloths and other luxury goods was conducted on a lavish scale. These were brought directly from Glasgow, Edinburgh and elsewhere, and this practice inhibited the evolution of a merchant class in the Isles. More importantly, it contributed greatly to the Isles' impoverishment, as a very substantial part of the annual financial product of the islands was constantly draining away, with little or no reinvestment and no large-scale improvement.

The concentration of great wealth in the hands of a few landowners encouraged this process. MacLeod of Dunvegan's income in 1644 was calculated at £15,000, MacDonald of Sleat's at £10,000 and Clanranald's at £9,000. Frances Shaw has pointed out the contrast between these and the earnings, at about that time, of the Orcadian landlords. In 1653 only eight landlords in Orkney had incomes in excess of £1,000, and none earned more than £2,000. It is interesting to note that in Shetland, an environment more readily comparable with the Western Isles than Orkney's large-scale landholdings were also the norm with, consequently, enormous earnings accruing.

Within a few centuries the greed for more money, to be spent elsewhere, led to the clearances. People were removed from the land, often under conditions of the greatest hardship, so that its capacity to earn would not be hindered by its need to sustain. To be fair, it must be admitted that the causes of the clearances were complex and many, but all of them might have been set aside if the traditional loyalties of the clans to their leaders and the duties and responsibilities of the leaders to their clans had been maintained. Rarely has a people been so thoroughly and so wretchedly betrayed by those whom they had loved and served so well.

Medieval

The seeds of the clearances lie in the commercialisation of the relationship between the landowners and the tenants. During the Lordship of the Isles that relationship was one of service and dependence. In return for their services, usually military, the members of the clan were provided for out of their chief's bounty. In turn they fed and housed him and his retinue on his progress through his lands and provided for his household in taxes of food and drink. He patronised the local craftsmen and supported traditional professions, notably the medical profession and the bards and *seanachaidh,* literally 'storyteller', but meaning 'historian'. The economy was largely closed and self-sustaining, although it was certainly at a low level. The price of raising that level was the destruction of the last elements of the Celtic way of life. It would be easy to romanticise this and to suggest that the process was one of the triumphs of money and greed over loyalty and devotion, but that would not be wholly true. It is doubtful if the life of an Iron Age peasant or a vassal of the Lordship period was one whit better or more severe than the lives of those who came thereafter.

In Ireland, after the Elizabethan wars, Celtic nobility was exiled and the peasantry faced largely the same trials and hardships as those encountered a century later in the Western Isles. The sense of loss at the passing of the old regime is expressed in remarkably similar ways by two seventeenth-century poets, one Irish, the other Scots. Raftery, the Irish poet, wrote (the author's translation):

> I am Raftery the poet
> full of hope and love
> with eyes without light
>   [he was blind]
> with a silence without disturbance
> going back over my journey

> (his life)
> by the light of my heart
> tired and weary now
> at the end of my way
> look at me now
> with my face to the wall
> playing my music
> to empty pockets.

Roderick Morison, the Scottish poet and harpist — who was also blind — described Dunvegan Castle, now that its new laird, Roderick MacLeod, spent all his time and money in Lowland Scotland, in these terms:

> Echo is dejected in the hall
> where music was want to sound
> in the place resorted to be
>   poet-bands
> now without mirth or pleasure or drinking,
> without merriment or entertainment
> without the passing round of
>   drinking horns
> in quick succession
> without feasting, without liberality
> to men of learning
> without dalliance, or voice raised
> in tuneful song.
> (From *The Blind Harper — An Clairsair Dall,* by W. Mathieson, 1970).

With the passing of the old order the Western Isles left behind them their prehistoric traditions and entered upon the Modern Age.

The traditions of any people are preserved in two separate but related ways. The first lies in the oral traditions which are handed down from generation to generation and which preserve vignettes of the past, often in the most incredable detail. Of their nature they deal with the unusual or the unexpected. It is a truism that the commonplace is not memorable. One such unusual event preserved in the vernacular memory of the Outer Isles is the sundering of Baleshare from the coast of North Uist. Beveridge records that on the night a woman, the last person to cross the causeway, departed Baleshare for the 'mainland' of North Uist. That night a severe storm breached the causeway which then rapidly eroded. The woman's name is known, and local people can point out her descendants. In cases like this there is absolutely no need to doubt the veracity of the tradition. Crawford alone amongst modern scholars has actively sought out such gems of preserved wisdom in his attempts to trace the settlement history of areas of North Uist, and this he has managed to some degree.

One of the modern tragedies of the Outer Isles is the gradual loss of these traditions to a largely uncaring generation. There are of course exceptions. The young people of the North of Lewis, some years ago, conducted a study of the recent history of the area, under the able guidance of Annie MacDonald (now Mrs McSween) and collected and recorded a great deal of information. Other local efforts have taken place, but it is clear that a concerted effort is now needed because within the next few decades that generation whose memories constitute our last living links with the past will have gone to its just rewards.

Far less fragile are the traditions which are enshrined in the physical fabric of the islands. Traditional house types, peat cutting, seaweed gathering and so on, these traditions are still very visible in the Isles, and although subject to change and development, are unlikely to be lost.

Some traditions are, of course, involuntary. The pattern of arable agriculture is in large part determined by the land itself. That the same crops are being grown in largely the same ways as they have been for centuries does not reflect a deliberate choice on the part of the growers, rather it bears mute testimony to the poverty of the natural resources. In animal husbandry sheep have come to replace cattle to an extent, but their export as the main cash crop of the islands continues a pattern established in the Iron Age. Similarly, televisions, CB radios and the like may have replaced the fine cloths and jewellery of earlier times as the luxury imports of the islands, but the pattern of expenditure outside the Isles remains unchanged. Given the same subsistence basis and a relatively unchanged economy, it is little wonder that the fundamental pattern of life itself in the Isles is, to the outsider, so redolent of times past.

The blackhouse, the typical Hebridean dwelling and at one time byre also, is one of the loveliest of the surviving relics of times past in the Isles. It varies in size from about 12m to 20m in length and from 5m to 8m in width. The walls are usually very thick, normally more than 1m thick, and comprise an outer and inner skin between which earth and clay have been packed. The walls are low, rarely higher than 1.5m, and the couples or opposed pairs of rafters rest directly on the walls. As will be appreciated, the absence of trees of any great size and the general scarcity of wood in the Isles has meant that rafters came to be made of the most unusual assortments of suitable-sized timbers. Regular squared timbers alternate with round tree trunks, many of them driftwood, and re-used timbers from staircases or from wrecked ships. Until very recently, and perhaps even still, people living in blackhouses could recount the history of their roof couples through repeated rebuildings over periods as long as three centuries. Many of these houses are now falling into disuse, and the once cherished roof timbers peer brokenly through rotting thatch. The blackhouse can often be seen close beside the new bungalows for which they were abandoned, but many have been refurbished and reroofed in slate or corrugated iron and continue to serve as domestic dwellings. One example has been taken into guardianship by the Scottish Development Department's Directorship of Historic Buildings and Monuments, at Arnol in Lewis, and this is worth a visit.

The blackhouse is part of the tradition of longhouse building common to the Atlantic seaboards of Ireland and Britain, and largely similar structures can be seen from Dingle in the south-west of Ireland to Yell in the north of Shetland. Its widespread distribution and lengthy survival suggest that its design is uniquely suited to its environment. Its long, low profile, with squat roof, absence of gables and rounded corners, leaves the Atlantic gales with little to gain purchase upon. The doors which are usually set opposite each other in the long walls can be opened on the sheltered side whichever way the wind blows. Perhaps most important of all, the materials of which they are composed are all gained locally. Stone and earth for walls, straw, reeds or heather for the thatch and also for the ropes which secure it, are all locally available. Originally the long house served as shelter both for beast and for man. The latter normally occupied the higher end and the beasts the lower from which drains ran out through the end walls. The economy of this arrangement in providing heating during the long winter and access to the beasts without the need to venture outside may have been sufficient recompense for the slight discomforts it must have caused both types of occupant. It is generally believed that the longhouse tradition was introduced to the British Isles, in general, by the Vikings. Part of the reason for believing this lies in the fact that all of the known pre-Viking dwellings were circular. Only the churches of the Early Christians were rectangular, and on several sites it is possible to show that the clerics themselves lived in circular houses. However, it is important to remember that most of these early houses are drystone-built and were roofed at least in part by corbelling. Thus stone structures were predisposed to circular plans, but the possibility that simple rectangular houses also existed must not be ruled out.

The use of seaweed as a fertiliser is clearly of great antiquity and in the recent past was of considerable importance. Seaweed, which was called seaware, contains more nitrogen and potassium than animal dungs but rather less phosphate. Its use was restricted to farms along the coast, and some beaches were better than others for collecting the seaweed. Its harvesting was usually a winter task, and a difficult and backbreaking task it is, as anyone who has attempted it will know. It is amazingly heavy for its volume, a factor which restricts its usage to the coastline farms. Normally seaweed is stacked in dump middens until it is needed for cultivation. Occasionally it was composted, with layers of soil or animal dung alternating with seaweed. Composting greatly enhanced its value as fertiliser but, if storms provided supplies of seaweed late in the winter or early spring, this was applied raw to the land. The remains of such dumps can still be seen on sites along the coast. Access to the beaches with rich annual hauls of weed was usually controlled, and strict rules governed the division of the spoils between local claimants. In the more recent past seaweed was collected for burning usually in the summer months, and the ashed debris was sold off the islands to the nascent chemical industry. Drying walls or stances also can still be seen along the west coast, where they survive as stone rows and low platforms. The modern visitor will see the commercial collection of seaweed from beaches in North Uist and elsewhere. Harvested by specially fitted tractors and carried by road in large and heavy lorries, the seaweed is used in the production of alginate plasticisers with a wide range of applications from the manufacture of ice-cream to casting powders for making false teeth. The use of seaweed in agriculture is very restricted now, although it can still be seen in potato beds along the coastal strip.

Peat cutting is a tradition as old in the Western Isles as the gathering of seaweed and one which, if anything, is even more likely to survive into the distant future. Peat cutting seems an apparently simple art to the uninitiated, but even brief acquaintance shows just how deceptive appearances can be. The process of peat cutting usually begins with the removal of the growing sod from the top of the bog. This is usually cut away with a large 'knife' especially developed for the task. These sods are placed on the cutaway area, or *gearraidh*, over the soil exposed by the previous cut. Then peats are cut with a specially adapted spade-like tool. The cutting edge of this tool is L-shaped, and it cuts the individual peat from the bank or bulk of the moss as well as from the next peat behind it. As each peat is cut, a second worker lifts it onto the top of the bog where it lies until it has dried sufficiently to be handled without falling apart. The next stage is to prop four or five peats together in such a way that the wind can circulate between them freely and hasten the drying process. When fully dry, they are either stacked on the bog for later transport or are carried home to be stacked beside the house. The peat stack itself is of some interest. The outer peats are normally laid in such a way as to shed the rain and keep the inner ones dry. It is possible even now to say roughly where one is in Scotland by the design of the peat stack and the shape of the peats. From the large deposits of peat ash visible in the exposed faces or eroding Iron Age middens along the coast it is clear that the use of peat as fuel is not new in the Western Isles. Indeed its use in the Bronze Age is attested, and it is probable that it was also used in the Neolithic Period, although confirmation of this is still wanting. However, with the likelihood that even when woods grew on the Isles they were not dense or particularly plentiful, it is probable that peat, formed in the bottoms of waterlogged hollows since the end of the Ice Age, was used from the earliest times by the inhabitants of the Western Isles.

It is possible to extend the list of archaic survivals in the Isles almost *ad nauseam.* The visitor may encounter relics whose antiquity ranges from that of the *cascrom* or footplough to landing craft of the Second World War. The former is still in use for cultivation, the latter he is likely to encounter pressed into service as an animal pen or a water trough. All is grist to the islands' timeless mill, and the sense of timelessness which this engenders is at the core of the Hebridean experience. One is left with the feeling that although the presence of man in the islands is amply attested by the surviving relics, it is the islands themselves which persist. Their latitude, climate, soils and geology have always dictated the terms on which human settlement could survive there, and these factors have not been tolerant of change. The modern passion for controlled preservation of the past or of the present environmental balance seems singularly presumptuous and pointless in the Isles. The past has survived there, visible in everything from the islands' ancient skeleton to the deserted houses of the last century. It survives without direct intervention, and it seems likely that the innate ability of the Isles to preserve their heritage will contine to succeed, not perhaps in the exact manner which modern taste and theory demand, but in accordance with its own unknown set of rules.

.BLacKHousEs

GAZETTEER of ARCHAEOLOGICAL SITES

The fact that we have listed sites does not confer on anyone the right to visit them. All of these sites are on privately owned land (with the exception of those in state ownership), and while access will very rarely be denied the visitor, it is polite to ask first. Furthermore it is vital that visitors respect the land over which they walk, or that freedom of access to the countryside we all enjoy will sooner or later be denied us. It ought not to be necessary to remind visitors not to allow their dogs to worry the sheep, to close gates after them, not to pull down stone walls and not to risk fires from discarded matches and cigarette ends. And yet, every year sees these old abuses continued, although fortunately they are not such a problem in the Western Isles as they have become elsewhere.

▷ A number of archaeological sites on the main islands are listed and described. These are organised in the order in which they occur along the main roads, without reference to their nature or date. Each major road segment is mapped and the sites are numbered on these maps and listed in numerical order in the gazetteer. For each site we have tried to indicate how accessible and how 'visible' they are. Accessibility is scaled from 1 to 5 as the sites go, from easily accessible to very inaccessible. Clearly this must be to some extent a subjective judgement, but we believe that sites coded 1 or 2 are readily accessible even to the elderly, while sites marked 5 may present a challenge to the relatively fit. The visual index is more difficult to explain and more subjective. In general it is compounded of the appearance of the site, both from the strictly archaeological and scenic viewpoints. Thus, of two sites which were equally interesting, archaeologically, we have chosen that which lies in the nicer setting. We would value readers' opinions on the utility and accuracy of our ratings.

If in the course of your journeying you locate something of archaeological interest, the people to contact are the National Museum of Antiquities of Scotland, Queen Street, Edinburgh (031-556 8921). If you see an archaeological site being damaged or destroyed, the relevant authority is the Directorate of Historic Buildings and Monuments, 3-11 Melville St., Edinburgh (031-226 2570). Local information is available from the Western Isles Tourist Organisation at South Beach Street, Stornoway (Telephone no. 3088), who will also assist with advice on accommodation. There are, of course, offices in the other islands. General advice on access to the Isles and on accommodation is available in Jemima Tindall's *Scottish Island Hopping*, published by Sphere Books. ◀

CHAPTER. 9

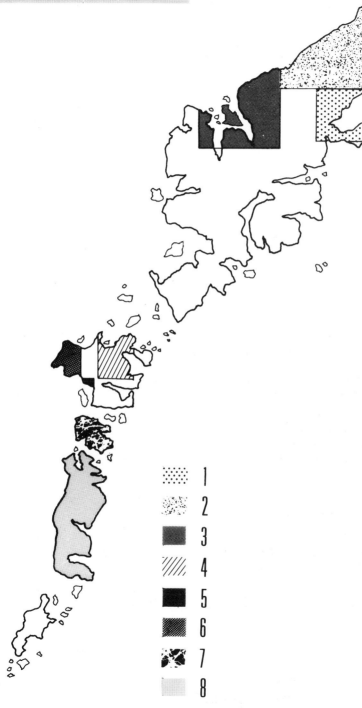

SITE.. DISTRIBUTION

BLOCK 1·8

1
2
3
4
5
6
7
8

SITE No 1   **LEWIS**
EYE CHURCH   CHURCH   NB 483 323

This roofless church near the neck of the Eye penninsula is set within a graveyard and beside the shore. Now two-chambered, it originally consisted of the larger (18.8m by 5.1m) eastern chamber probably built in the fourteenth century to which the smaller (7.0m by 5.1m) western chamber was added sometime around 1500 A.D. The original entrance, a roundheaded door in the south wall, is now bricked up. The architecture is uninspiring and there has clearly been some remodelling of doorways, etc.

The importance of this site lies in the marvellous 16th-century carved grave slab, carved in memory of Margaret Mackinnon, mother of John, the last abbot of Iona, who died in 1503. The inscription is now illegible.

Visual index 1.   Accessibility 1.

This site lies on the Eye Peninsula some six miles from Stornoway and is east of the A866 just beyond Garrabost. The site is almost totally destroyed, with only an approximately circular setting of seven of its kerb stones still *in situ*, together with a number of stones which seem to have formed part of the chamber. Despite its ruinous state this is still well worth a visit.

Visual index 2.   Accessibility 3.

▷

▷

▷

▷

▷

▷

▷

▷

This site is on the Eye Peninsula, in Loch an Dun, near Lower Bable, approached via the A866 and a side road. It is very ruinous, consisting of a roughly circular mass of stone ranging from 1.2m to 1.5m high covering a small islet which is connected to the land by a manmade causeway 2.7m wide and about 27m long. Parts of the outer wall face can be seen, close to the water level. The dun, which seems to have had a solid wall, was about 15m in diameter.

Visual index 2.   Accessibility 2.

SITE No 4   LEWIS
COLL CHAMBERED CAIRN NB 450 382

This site lies in moorland west of the
B895 about 3½ miles from Stornoway. It
consists of a cairn just over 15m in
diameter and 1m high. The body of the
cairn is in poor condition and has clearly
been disturbed, but the remains of a
roughly circular chamber, about 2m in
diameter, can be seen somewhat east of
its centre. Two or three large slabs lying
partly in the chamber may be all that
survive of its roofing. It is not possible to
identify the entrance passage to the
tomb, but the inclusion of some large
slabs and boulders in the cairn debris on
the south-west side may be all that
remains of it.

Visual index 2.   Accessibility 3.

SITE No 5   LEWIS
GRESS CHAMBERED CAIRN NB 472 438

This site lies west of the B895, some 7½
miles from Stornoway. It is set on a
hillside north of Gress River and
commands a wide view of the moorland,
the Minch and the mountains of the
mainland beyond. Its location is unusual
in that it seems to be set on a platform
which is at least partially manmade,
material having been removed from the
uphill side and redeposited on the
downhill slope to extend an existing level
space. The cairn measures 28m
north–east to south–west and about
23m across. It is almost 3m high. It has
undergone some damage, and the big
slabs in the south-west quadrant are
probably the remains of the passage and
chamber. Part of the kerb is visible
around the south-western edge.

Visual index 2.   Accessibility 3/4.

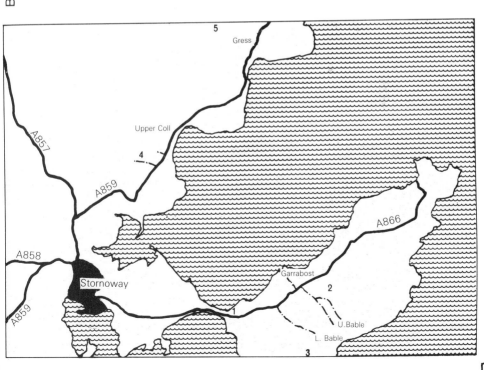

This magnificent standing stone is situated on the north slope of a gentle hill about a quarter of a mile north-west of the fifteenth milestone on the A858, from Stornoway to Ness. It is fully 5.7m high (almost 19ft) by 2m wide by 1m thick at its base.

Visual index 1.   Accessibility 1.

SITE No 7   **LEWIS**
TEAMPULL PHEADAIR   RUINED CHURCH   NB 379 550
(midden and early crofting landscape)

The ruined church at this site consists of a grass-covered rectangular mound, almost 12m long. The church may have consisted of two chambers — nave (approximately 7.5m long) and chancel. Its date is unknown, but at least part of the site must be of the Early Christian Period.

On the coast adjacent to this side is the point called Rubha Bhlanisgaidh, and in the eroding, low cliff face a typical midden can be seen, rich in animal bone, sea shells and pottery, all set in a matrix of dark soil. The date of this example is unknown, but it is likely to be in the Late Iron Age to Medieval Period.

North-eastwards from this site may be seen the remains of old crofts and houses extending from the coast inland to where they meet the modern croftlands.

Visual index 1.   Accessibility 4.

SITE No 8   **LEWIS**
STEINACLEIT   CHAMBERED CAIRN   NB 396 540

This very fragmented tomb lies off the A857 near Shadar on the north-west side of Lewis. It consists of a kerb of ten vertically set slabs surrounding a very denuded cairn. This originally measured about 15m in diameter, and fragments of the burial chamber may still be identified in the set slabs which lie close to the cairn's centre.

Visual index 1.   Accessibility 2.

SITE No 9   LEWIS
TEAMPULL MHOLUIDH   NB 518 652
CHURCH

The restored church on this site is of more interest for its name than its architecture, although the latter is anomalous. It measures 13.4m by 5.4m internally and has a sacristry at its north-east corner, entered from the church, while a small chapel abuts its south-east corner. The chapel is entered from without by a door in its west wall, and a narrow slit window looks into the east end of the church. The east wall of sacristy, church and chapel are of a single build.

The curious east window with its pointed rear arch and semicircular outer arch is an artefact of the somewhat heavy-handed reconstruction. The construction date is unknown but unlikely to have been earlier than the fourteenth century.

Myth and legend attend the church from its very name (see Chapter 6, p. 66 for details) to the curious, relatively recent practices noted there. Martin — a traveller to the isles about 1695 — commented on the association between the church and a Hallowe'en Ritual of sacrifice to a sea god called Shony. Local memory indicates that lunatics were cured by being made to lie on its alter overnight!

The church has acted as a repository for many querns and grinding stones. Its font was brought from North Rona at the time of its reconstruction, and a stone cross may also have come from that island.

Visual index 1.   Accessibility 2.

SITE No 10   LEWIS
TEAMPULL RONAIDH   NB 518 652
RUINED CHURCH

The ruins of this church — dedicated to St Ronan — consist of an irregular stony mound roughly 8m by 6m. It is sited, in croftland, on a low hill about 500m north-east of Teampull Mholuidh. The site commands sweeping views to the east and west. Local tradition suggests that this was the first church to be built in Lewis.

Visual index 4.   Accessibility 4.

block 2

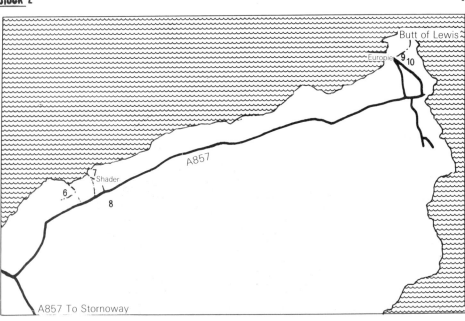

SITE No 11   **LEWIS**
DUN LOCH AN DUNA   BROCH   NB 286 474

This broch lies on a narrow, low spit of land jutting out into the north-east corner of Loch an Duna at Bragor, on the A858. It measures 16m in external diameter and its wall, over 3.5m thick, encloses an area some 9m in diameter. The outer wall face is battered slightly and pierced by a narrow entrance (approximately 0.75m wide) on the south-east side. The south wall of the entrance has a door check, and a barhole is visible in the northern wall. The entrance is protected by a guard cell which opens into the south wall of the entrance, now largely blocked with rubble. A second cell is visible, though partly destroyed on the north-west side, and a third can be detected in the rubble at the north. A gallery runs through the thickness of the wall from the north-east, clockwise to the north-west.

   A scarcement, or ledge, projects out from the internal wall at a height of about 3m above the ground level outside the entrance.

Visual index 1.   Accessibility 1.

SITE No 12   **LEWIS**
RUBHA NA BEIGHRE   PROMONTORY FORT   NB 235 474

The promontory of Rubha na Beighre is a sea-girt rocky spine about 30m high and measuring about 210m long by 90m wide. It is joined to the land by a narrow neck across which a massive stone wall has been built, thus fortifying the promontory. The wall must have been very strong, its tumbled spread now measuring almost 9m wide in places. Entrance was gained around the south end of the wall where a gap of some 4m was left between the wall end and the edge of the cliff. That this was a readily defensible entrance will be appreciated by anyone who tries to negotiate it in a strong wind even today.

   A shallow ditch with low banks on either side lies to the landward of the wall and may originally have been part of the defences. It is not known whether the internal ruined structures were contemporaneous with the fortification.

Visual index 4.   Accessibility 5.

Situated on a rocky knoll just south-west of the township of Carloway off the A858, this site is one of the most spectacular monuments in the Western Isles, despite the fact that it is rather incomplete. The broch is over 9m high, on its west side consisting of a double wall some 3.3m thick enclosing an area 7.6m in diameter. The entrance opens to the north-west and is 0.9m high and 1.1m wide though it opens to 1.5m wide at the door checks. A guard cell opens onto the south wall of the entrance passage; this cell measures 1.5m by 2.4m in plan, and in turn opens onto a second cell to which it is joined by a passage some 1.5m long (passage now blocked off). The second cell is 2.9m by 1.7m in plan, and it extends a further 4.6m to the east under the stairs to the galleries. It has a door leading to the broch's interior. Two further entrances are to be seen in the northern wall.

Opposite the entrance to the broch a low doorway gives access to a short (2m) alcove, on the left, and to the stairway to the galleries, on the right. The galleries spiral upwards within the thickness of the wall, which is in fact two separate walls, keyed together by the large slabs which make up the floor of the galleries. Since the outer wall is strongly battered, the width of the galleries diminishes with height, ranging from 0.8m wide in the lowest level to 0.3m in the uppermost.

The scarcement, 2.1m above ground level and 0.25m wide, is constructed by slight corbelling of the lower level. Above the scarcement the internal wall is vertical. The vertical array of window-like openings over the internal door is a device to reduce the weight to be borne by the lintel slabs of the door opes.

Visual index 1.   Accessibility 2.

SITE No 14   LEWIS
CALLANISH   CHAMBERED CAIRN, STONE CIRCLE   NB 213 330
                          AND STONE ALIGNMENTS

Situated adjacent to the village of Callanish and approached by a by-road off the
A858, this site is amongst the most spectacular in the British Isles. It consists of a
chambered tomb set within a stone circle from which a series of lines of stone radiate
to the north, south, east and west. All of the stones used are large thin slabs of
gneiss, and the slab set at the centre of the circle is some 5m high by 1.5m wide by a
mere 0.30m thick. This central slab forms the back of the cairn containing the
chambered tomb. This consists of two chambers separated by jamb stones and
entered by a passage some 2m long. One of the stone circle's uprights forms the north
corner of the entrance to the tomb, the south being formed of the drystone walling of
which the tomb walls are constructed throughout. Fragments of human bone were
recovered from this chamber when it was first revealed in 1857–8 by Sir James
Matheson following the removal of the five-foot-deep deposit of peat which had grown
up over the entire site since the time of its construction.
    The stone circle is about 11.25m in diameter and consists of thirteen orthostats
(standing stones) averaging 2.3m high. From its northern side two roughly parallel
lines of stones almost 8m apart run north from the circle for a distance of more than
80m. Ten stones, averaging just over 2m in height, make up the western alignment,
whilst the eastern consists of nine stones, averaging almost 1.7m in height. An
apparently similar but smaller pair of alignments seems to have run south from the
circle, but only one stone of the east line survives, while there are five in the western
line, averaging 1.7m high. Single lines of orthostats radiate east and west from the
circle also, four stones only in each case.
    The whole impression of the site is one of great complexity, and this has prompted
recent claims that the site was used as an ancient astronomical device, a claim for
which there is very little supporting evidence. However, recent excavations have
shown that the complexity of the site is real enough. A considerable complexity of
building history and many episodes of site use which are not represented in the visible
remains was thus revealed, and the publication of the excavation report in due course
should do much to help our understanding of this magnificent site.

Visual index 1.   Accessibility 1.

CALLANISH

STONE

NB 213 330

These three sites lie within a half mile of each other and about one mile south of Garrinahine, a township situated on the A858 some twelve miles west of Stornoway.

Site 1. This site is about a mile from Garrinahine and some 250m west of the B8011. It is situated on the northern slope of a low hill and commands fine views in all directions except southwards. It consists of an outer circle of five large slabs, ranging from 2m to 3m in height. This surrounds a rough circle of boulders within which is set a low slab, about 0.6m high. The outer circle is some 10m in diameter, the inner, boulder circle being just under 4m in diameter.

Visual index 1.   Accessibility 2.

Site 2. This site lies about half a mile south-east of site 1 on the northern shoulder of a hill called Airidh nam Bidearan. It seems to consist of two concentric circles, the outer some 16m in diameter and consisting of five stones, the inner some 9m in diameter.

Visual index 1.   Accessibility 2.

Site 3. This site lies some 300m west of site 2, and consists of a circle of tall thin slabs some 20m in diameter surrounding a small cairn. The slabs are up to 3m high while the cairn, some 8.5m in diameter and lying on the eastern half of the circle, may contain a burial cist.

Visual index 1.   Accessibility 2.

This site lies on a small islet in Loch Baravat on Great Bernera, approached via the B8059, and a side road. It consists of an oval galleried dun 12.2m by 9.2m internally which is connected to the loch shore by a manmade causeway some 30m in length. Only the northern quarter is well preserved where the wall survives to a height of 3.3m and is some 2.4m thick. A scarcement is visible on the internal wall face above which part of a gallery may be seen. A lower gallery is also visible with a chamber at intermediate height. The greater part of the dun is obscured by the later building which lies partly within and partly over the wall.

Visual index 1.   Accessibility 5.

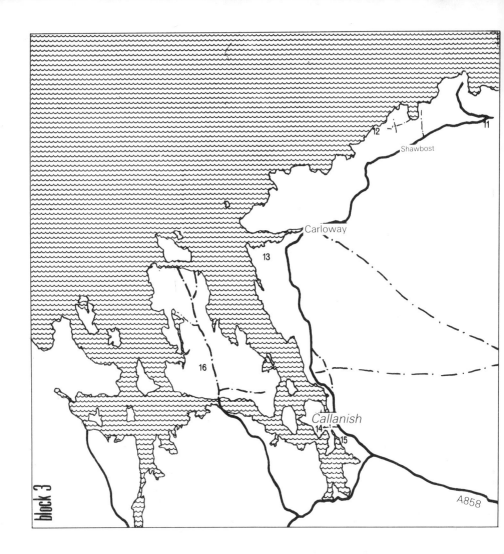

SITE No 17

DUN CROMORE   GALLERIED DUN   NB 400 206

This site lies about 46m from the west shore of Loch Cromore just south of the township of Cromore, approached via the A859 and B8060. It is connected to the loch shore by a causeway which is now for the most part under water. The site consists of an oval galleried dun measuring 15.8m by 13.2m which occupies the south-eastern part of the island. The north-western part has been converted to a courtyard by an encircling arc of walling, open to the north where the causeway adjoins. Entry to the dun was from the courtyard, though the northern side of the entrance is now destroyed. The gallery can be clearly seen within the thickness of the wall. Early visitors recorded an upper gallery, but no trace of this or the access stairway survives.

Visual index 2.   Accessibility 2

St Clements Church at Rodil in Harris is the architectural gem of the Western Isles, and even the fact that the islands' architecture is in general depressingly poor does not detract from the splendour of St Clements.

The church is located on an uneven, rocky knoll overlooking Loch Rodil and consists of a cruciform church with a tower attached at its west end. The church is 25m long, with no division between nave and chancel, although at the eastern end a strip 3.0m long E/W is raised a little above the general floor level. The transepts are set somewhat out of alignment with each other and average 4.8m by 3.0m internally. Entrance to the church is by a door in the north wall. The window opes are of three types. The first are simple lintelled opes; the second are narrow, cusp headed windows with freestone dressings grooved for glazing; and the third group consists of the large, east window and one other in the south-east of the choir. Despite these variations there is no reason to believe that all are not of the same early sixteenth-century date.

The tower rises some 20m to the parapet above (and within) which the pyramidal roof rises. The foundations of the tower are set some 4m above the floor of the nave, to accommodate the rocky outcrop on which it is built. Entry to the tower is via a doorway in the centre of the west wall of the nave which gives access to a mural staircase rising to the lowest floor of the tower. This lowest chamber is a simple room, some 4m square, and a second mural staircase rises thence to the first-floor chamber. Ascent beyond this was presumably by ladder or wooden staircase.

ORNAMENTATION

External ornament at St Clements is concentrated on the tower and begins at a string course 14m above the ground. The string course is corbelled and breaks upwards at the corners and at the centres of the wall faces. At the centres a frame is thus formed within which sculpted panels are inserted. On the north wall is a bull's head, at the west; a figure, probably St Clement himself, with a bull's head beneath his feet; on the east wall a beautifully vulgar nude figure, with a child, set in a crouched attitude in blatant display of her vagina. This is a type of decoration commonly found on early Irish churches, which are called *Shiela-na-gigs*. The origin or significance is obscure, but an approximately contemporaneous sketch shows worshippers entering a church while the satanic figures which follow them — representative of the evils of life — are distracted by the charms of a Shiela-na-gig, allowing the faithful a respite from trial and temptation while at their prayers.

Beneath the panel in the west wall face are two male figures, one in kilt and plaid, the other in jerkin, trunks and hose. Above the string course the corners of the tower are moulded; they bear a 'quirked edge' roll and fillet, in the jargon of the architectural historian. This is broken, at each corner, at a level 3m above the string course by a projecting bull's head. Above that the edge roll continues, without the fillet.

The head of the east window is a pointed arch containing a wheel with six spokes. The lower part is divided in three lights (or panels) with trefoil heads. It is ornamented with dogtooth on the label and nailhead on the tracery. At the stops and finial human heads are carved in freestone. The south-east window in the choir also had a painted head but this is now infilled.

THE TOMBS

Alexander Macleod (Lord of Dunvegan 1528) tomb.
This is undoubtedly one of Scotland's finest sculptured tombs. Set in the south wall of the choir, it consists of a recessed semicircular arch, the outer face of which is contained within a triangular moulding. On the outer face, nine panels of carved

figures are arranged in an arc between the moulding and the arch. The top centre panel shows the Saviour on a cross held by a seated figure of the Father. The remaining panels display the twelve apostles, some of whom are identified by abbreviated forms of their names — 'Mat' for 'Matthew', for example — some, like Saint Andrew, being identified by the symbols with which they are associated.

The face of the recess bears three horizontal rows of panels. The top row consists of three panels with angels in the outer two flanking another in the centre who is blowing a curved trumpet. This possibly represents Gabriel summoning the dead on Judgement Day. Five panels occupy the central row of which the central panel displays the Virgin and Child. This is flanked by panels displaying bishops, one of whom is identified as St Clement. The outermost panels contain a castle, on the left, and a galley under sail; both motifs from the Macleod coat of arms. The bottom row shows a hunting scene — on the left; Michael and Satan weighing the souls of the departed in the centre, and an inscription on the right. The inscription translates, roughly, as 'This place was composed [i.e. this tomb was built] by Alexander, son of William Macleod, Lord of Dunvegan, A.D. 1528.'

The figure on the tomb is armoured and holds a sword, by the hilt, perpendicularly between the legs. Carved lions lie at the head and foot of the figure, that at the head being largely destroyed.

The second tomb is immediately west of the transept and consists of a recessed area 2m long and 0.3m deep under a semicircular arch, the outer face of which is contained within a triangular moulding. Between the arch and the moulding is a crucifixion scene. The face of the recess bears an illegible Gothic inscription. The figure is armoured, the feet resting on two hounds with another hound beside the head.

- ● St Circle
- ● St Stone
- ■ Dun
- ◎ Broch
- x Church
- ▬ Teampull
- 0 Cairn

LEWIS ∵ HARRIS

Spot Map

BLocK 4

This site lies on an island in Loch an Sticer, just east of the B893 road and immediately south of the road which departs the latter for the Berneray ferry. It is approached by a splendid, manmade causeway which averages 3m in width and curves out to the island, from the northern shore of the loch. The loch is now tidal, its level controlled by the valve sited under the bridge which carries the Berneray ferry road, but it is unlikely to have been tidal at the time of the broch's construction. The broch is approximately 18m in external diameter and has been greatly damaged by the insertion of a later rectangular structure, which is probably of sixteenth-century date. Local tradition identifies this as the residence of the baillie of MacDonald of Sleat, a man called Uisdean MacGuilleasbuig. Little of the broch's original organisation can now be seen, though the wall is well preserved on the south side where it is up to 3m high.

Visual index 1.   Accessibility 1.

SITE No 20   NORTH UIST
DUN TORCUILL   BROCH   NB 889 738

This site lies in Loch an Duin, in the north angle of the junction between the A865 and the road, to Lochportain and Cheese Bay. The broch is sited on an island some 32m south of a promontory on the west side of the loch. Although it is somewhat dilapidated, it is the best example of a broch on North Uist. It is connected with the promontory by a 2m-wide causeway which approaches it in a broad curve, taking advantage of a natural outcrop along its course. The interior of the broch is roughly circular and 11.5m in diameter. It is so filled with fallen stone that the entrances to the ground galleries cannot be seen. The galleries themselves are visible, mainly on the north side, through the collapse of the wall. The thickness of the wall varies from 2.5m to almost 4m, and although it is in part very ruinous, it yet survives to a height of between 3m and 3.5m. The entrance passage is on the north-west side but only its north wall is now visible. The remains of several irregularly shaped enclosures of unknown date, though later than the broch, can be seen abutting it.

Visual index 2.   Accessibility 4.

SITE No 21   NORTH UIST
BARPA NA FEANNAG   NB 856 721
CHAMBERED CAIRN

This site is most difficult of access and not terribly exciting in itself but is included here for those who like a challenging walk. It lies about 2km south of the A865 and just east of Loch nan Geireann. The site consists of a cairn 50m long and about 14m wide, and slabs of what must be its chamber are visible at its south-east end. Less than 1km to the north-east, on the south slopes of the hill, called Maari, are three further cairns set in a sheltered spot below a cliff. These all have recent shielings built atop them. The two smaller mounds are oval and about 3m high and may, in fact, be Bronze Age burial cairns. The eastern mound has the appearance of a long cairn, though like the site at Barpa na Feannag it is not possible to say exactly what type it is. If the walker returns along the Bealach Maari, the path through the saddle between Maari and Crogary Mor, he will also see the standing stone which marks the south west-side of the saddle. Returning towards the road, the site of a dun in Loch Aonghais can be seen. The view from the top of Maari, south and eastwards out over the loch-studded peat-covered moorland, provides one of the best examples of the knock-and-lochan landscape which the islands afford. For that alone the walk is more than worth the effort.

Visual index 1.   Accessibility 5.

SITE No 22   NORTH UIST
LOCH HUNDER   DUNS   NF 905 635

These sites are probably best approached along the west foot of the North and South Lee hills, to which access can be gained from the A867, some 2km west of Loch Maddy. The first of these two duns is sited on a small island near the east shore of Loch Hundar to which it is connected by a causeway. This dun is markedly oval in plan, measuring roughly 12m by 10m in external dimension. The wall varies from 1.5m to almost 3m in thickness and contains at least one chamber, on its northern side. The causeway from the eastern shore is about 36m long and 2m wide. From the dun, a second causeway runs out to an island some 45m distant. This second site, although called a dun, is little more than an annexe to the first. It is only slightly fortified with a slab-built wall less than 1m high along its eastern edge, while the remains of a slight, stone wall can be seen across the access route from the causeway. From this second site a farther causeway runs to the further shore of the loch. If the site is visited when the causeways are under water, the intrepid visitor should be warned that the causeways make several sharp changes in direction.

Visual index 3.   Accessibility 4/5.

This site lies on the north-west shoulder of Ben Langass and is readily visible from the A867 which passes the foot of the hill. It is probably the best preserved of the chambered tombs of North Uist; its cairn, measures about 24m in diameter and stands to a height of 4.5m. The remains of its kerb of small slabs can be seen in places. The entrance passage, on the east side, leads into a small polygonal chamber about 3m long and 2m wide. The walls of the chamber are made of upright slabs interspersed with drystone walling, and they reach a height of over 2m. The roof is formed by two large lintels with a third placed above to cover the gap between them. The entrance passage is 3.5m long and, like the chamber, is built of a mixture of upright slabs and drystone walling. It too is roofed with lintel slabs. Although it is somewhat congested with fallen stones, it is still possible to get into the tomb and well worth the effort involved; but remember that a torch or candle is vital. Finds retrieved from this site after investigation in 1911 include Neolithic pottery, flint objects, Bronze Age Beaker pottery and cremated human bone. A second chamber on the North side of the tomb was said to have been accessible last century, but this is now all but invisible.

Visual index 1.   Accessibility 1.

The stone circle of Pobull Fhinn lies on the south-west side of Ben Langass, overlooking Loch Langass, from which it is only about 100m distant. It is irregularly oval in shape and measures 37m east to west, and 30m north to south. It sits on a platform which seems to have been partly manmade. The north end of the plateau is cut back into the slope of the hill, while the south end projects out over the normal hill slope. The stones of the circle seem to be placed on a slight bank, especially on its south side. A total of 24 stones and boulders can be seen, but it is not clear how many of these actually belong in the circle. The stones average about a metre in height, but some may have originally been higher. A fallen slab on the south-west side, now almost overgrown, measures 2.5m in length.

While visiting the circle the opportunity to visit Langass Lodge should not be missed. It provides excellent meals in an atmosphere of warm Hebridean hospitality.

Visual index 1.   Accessibility 2.

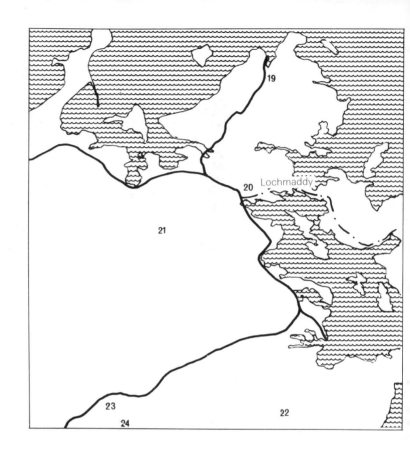

SITE No 25   NORTH UIST
CROANAVAL CENTRED ON NF 830 630
CAIRNS AND STONE CIRCLE

The hill of Craonaval, which is notable
for the number of monuments it bears,
lies just south of the B894, from Clachan
to Sidinish about 3km from Clachan.
Two large slabs are set on the north-
western of the hill's two summits. These
are known as Leac a Mhiosachan. North-
west from these, and about 250m away,
are two large but badly damaged cairns.
The largest is about 20m in diameter and
2.5m high. The other is only slightly
smaller. These two cairns are as likely to
be Bronze Age as Neolithic in date, and
only excavation could now resolve their
nature and date.

About 200m south of these two, closer to the summit of the hill and somewhat to the west, is a further cairn which may have been a passage grave, but this also is greatly damaged and it is impossible to be confident of this. Some of the stones of its kerb survive, and these suggest that the original cairn was about 15m in diameter, although cairn material now spreads beyond this limit. Near the centre of the cairn is a large square stone cist about 1.25m square. East of that is what appears to be the chamber, consisting of two rectangular chambers made of orthostatic slabs. Large slabs lie nearby and may have formed the roofing to the chamber.

Returning northwards, past the two cairns mentioned above, and some 100m further on, lies a simple stone circle which seems well preserved.

Visual index 2   Accessibility 2.

SITE No 26   NORTH UIST
TEAMPULL NA TRIONAID   CHURCH   NF 818 605

The ruins of this church are situated on the summit of a low hill on the north-west side of the Carinish peninsula. The remains consist of the church, which measures 6.5m by 18.5m, adjoining which, on its north side, and connected to it by a vaulted passage, is a second structure, 4m by 7m, which seems to have been a house rather than an ecclesiastical building. The church, dedicated to the Holy Trinity, is of little architectural merit and is in a very poor state indeed. Its interior is destroyed — from the archaeological viewpoint — by the repeating insertions of burials, and is now, moreover, badly overgrown. The church, together with all of Carinish and four pennylands of Illeray, was granted, in 1389, by Godfrey, Lord of the Isles, to the Monastery of Saint John at Inchaffray, Perthshire. Rather it is more correct to say that he confirmed this grant, originally made by his mother's aunt. It was again confirmed by Donald, Lord of the Isles, in 1410, but by the middle of the next century it was listed amongst the lands of the Abbot of Iona. In 1601 the 'Battle of Carinish' took place between the MacLeods of Harris and the local MacDonalds, when the former went to take goods and cattle from the church precinct where they had been placed, 'as in a sanctuarie'.

Visual index 3.   Accessibility 1.

SITE No 27   NORTH UIST
CARINISH   STONE CIRCLE   NF 833 602

This once fine stone circle is actually cut by the A865 road and suffered considerably in a recent episode of road widening. It lies about 1.5km east of Carinish, but it can be hard to find in the overgrowing heather and the dumps of debris from the road widening. It measures 39m north to south and 41.5m east to west. The site was described by the Royal Commission (on Ancient and Historic Monuments) in 1915 as consisting of at least sixteen stones, of which ten were fallen. They ranged in height from 1m to 2.5m. The visitor may judge how much the site has suffered in the intervening years by trying to count the shattered stumps of stone which remain.

Visual index 4.   Accessibility 1.

SITE No 28   **NORTH UIST**
BARPA CARINISH   CHAMBERED CAIRN   NF 836 603

This cairn is visible from site no. 27, above and about 500m east of it, across a very broken stretch of moorland in which deep gullies are obscured by the dense growth of heather. The site is quite spectacular, over 50m long and 2m high. It is markedly trapezoidal in plan, being 21m wide at the east end, narrowing and tailing out into the peat at the west end. The remains of the chamber are visible, and one of the two horns of the cairn can be made out on the south side. The chamber must have opened out onto a wide shallow forecourt, now largely obscured. Some of the orthostatic slabs of the southern horn and of the north and south sides of the cairn can still be seen. The chamber now represented by six orthostats is about 5.5m long, but of course it may extend further in either direction; only excavation could reveal its true extent. Several large flat slabs can be seen scattered about at the east end. These may have been corbels or roofing lintels. Though archaeologically a little ambiguous, this is a lovely site, in a beautiful setting. We the authors first saw it while fishing in the loch to the west, the long, thin loch, from which position it was visible on the skyline, the grey mass of the cairn stones picked out against a gradually darkening sky.

Visual index 1.   Accessibility 2.

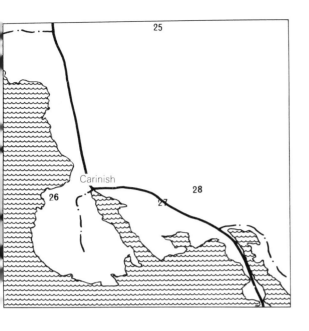

BLoCK 6

SITE No 29   NORTH UIST
CLACH MOR AN CHE   STANDING STONE AND CHAMBERED CAIRN   NF 769 661

The massive standing stone of this name is visible from many points along the A865
road north of Clachan. It stands about 20m from the sea at high tide and is 2.5m high,
1.2m wide and about 0.4m thick. Some 20m away can be seen the dilapidated
remains of Dun Na Carnaich, an almost square chambered cairn. This has been largely
destroyed by a trench which runs across it and which must have removed the inner
part of the chamber. Four large slabs along the north side of the cairn mark the line of
the facade. Seven orthostats of the chamber and/or passage can be seen running
south-west from the centre of the facade, but it is impossible, without excavation, to
suggest what its original form may have been. A visit to these sites provides an
excellent excuse, if such be needed, for a call upon the Westford Inn, the home of real
Hebridean hospitality and the only place where lunch can be had on the west side of
North Uist.

Visual index 2.   Accessibility 3.

SITE No 30   NORTH UIST
CLETTRAVAL   CHAMBERED LONG CAIRN AND WHEEL HOUSE   NF 749 713

The site of Clettraval lies close to the summit of the hill of that name and is clearly
visible from the side road, off the A865, which gives access to the radar station. The
cairn was of the long variety, but its west end has been destroyed in the construction
of an Iron Age wheel house. The cairn was originally wedge-shaped and 30m long,
with an impressive facade at the east end. The surviving, southern half of the facade
is 24m long so that the whole facade must have been about 50m wide. The chamber,
some 10.5m long, follows a somewhat curving path and consists of five
compartments constructed of orthostats throughout. The compartments were
separated from each other by sill stones. The excavation of the site produced a small
amount of cremated human bone and an even smaller number of burnt sheep or goat

bones, as well as a mass of Neolithic and Beaker pottery, all of which are now in the National Museum of Antiquities in Edinburgh.

Visual index 2.   Accessibility 2.

SITE No 31   NORTH UIST
TOWER   FOLLY   NF 731 751

At the point where the A856 turns east to run along the north coast, it rises up over the foot of Beinn Riabhach, and the traveller will be surprised to see below him on an island in Loch Scolpaig a tall octagonal tower complete with battlements. This is a Victorian folly, erected by Dr Alex MacLeod, who was known locally as An Dolair Ban. He was a chamberlain of the MacDonald estates and had an intense interest in their heritage, a heritage to which he can now be said to have contributed! His also is the fine Latin cross erected in the graveyard about 1.5km to the south, near Kilpheddir. From the site of the cross there are fine views seaward to the Haiskier Islands and on a clear evening to the distant peaks of St Kilda.

Visual index 2.   Accessibility 1.

SITE No 32   NORTH UIST
CAISTEAL ODAIR   NF 731 766
                PROMONTORY FORT

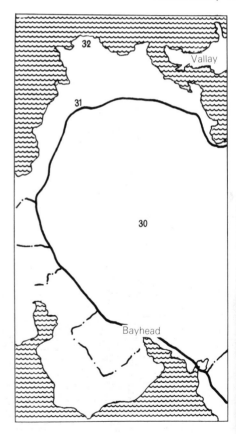

The walk to Caisteal Odair is rather long but not unpleasant. It may be approached either from Scolpaig or Griminish, and it lies at the extreme north-west corner of North Uist, just north of Griminish Point. It consists of a promontory protected on the seaward side by steep cliffs, and on the landward side by a drystone wall some 110m in length and over 3m thick. It is now greatly reduced, being nowhere more than 0.5m high, but the entrance can still be seen, about 30m from the south-western end. The entrance passage curved through the thickness of the wall, giving it an overall length of 4.5m. Inside the wall are the remains of at least two circular huts and a small cairn, but of course it is not possible, without excavation, to say whether these are contemporaneous with the defending wall.

Visual index 1.   Accessibility 5.

L O C K ⑦

SITE No 33   **BENBECULA**
GRAMISDALE STONES   TWO STONE CIRCLES   NF 825 563, & 825 554

Both of these sites are marked as standing stones on the Ordnance Survey 1 in
50,000 map. They lie east of the A865. The northern one overlooks the point where
the causeway from North Uist joins Benbecula. The second site lies 1km south of the
first and can be approached by the track from Gramsdale to Flodda. Only a single
standing stone survives at each site, but at the northern one a further nine fallen slabs
can be traced in the vegetation, spread out along one half of a circle of 26m
approximately. At the southern circle only two fallen stones survive, together with the
standing stone to mark the site of the circle. Both sites present pleasant views over
the rock-studded strait to Grimsay and North Uist.

Visual index 1.   Accessibility 2.

▷

SITE No 34   BENBECULA
DUN BUIDHE   NF 794 546
DUN AND LATER BUILDINGS

This site was originally on the outermost of two sall islands on the north side of Loch Dun Mhurchaidh — to which access can be gained through Knock Rolum township. Causeways had joined the outer, south island to the inner, and this to the loch shore, but lowering of the water level has rejoined the inner island to the shore and revealed the causeway throughout, much of it now on dry land. Both causeways are substantial constructions, being over 2m wide in places. The wall of the dun follows the outline of the island and was presumably built at the water's edge, though it now stands up to 12m to 15m from it. Of the early building within the wall, only traces can now be seen at the centre of the dun. The remainder of the internal area is taken up with the long houses of a (probably) seventeenth-century township, or 'baile'. It is interesting to note that the circumstances of the seventeenth-century A.D. were sufficiently similar to those of the Iron Age to cause the sites of the latter to be re-used, and in quite a similar fashion to their original use. The wall of the dun is very dilapidated, and little impression of its original form and size can now be gained.

Visual index 1.   Accessibility 2.

SITE No 35   BENBECULA
STIARAVAL   NF 813 527
PASSAGE GRAVE

This site lies about 1km east of the A865 and 50m north of Loch Nan Clachan, in an extensive area of rough moorland. The cairn has suffered considerably from stone robbing and does not seem to be higher than 1.25m, at best. However, the chamber and passage survive reasonably intact. The monument is encumbered with small shelters, presumably erected for sheep, and even the chamber seems to have been used as a shelter, with loose slabs arranged on its northern side for this purpose. The chamber is approximately 4m in diameter, roughly circular, and constructed of large orthostatic slabs, of which five, making up about three-quarters of its circuit, are still in place. The north-east side of the passage also survives. It is 4m long and made up of two orthostats of which one is over 3m long. There are up to twenty large slabs lying about in the area of the chamber, and these are probably the corbels from its roof. It is little short of tragic to see such a beautiful site reduced to such a state.

Visual index 2.   Accessibility 4.

SITE No 36   BENBECULA
AIRIDH NA HAON OIDHCHE NF 817 525
CHAMBERED LONG CAIRN

This site lies about 500m further east than the site 35 above. It is on the top of a low hill and forms a quite distinct feature in this barren landscape. It is difficult to say exactly what type of cairn this is, not because it is too ruinous but because it is too well preserved! Archaeologists, like farmers, are rarely content with their lot. The cairn is oval, 17 by 14m, and up to 4m high. With so few structural stones visible through the cairn, it is hard to know how the chamber/s, passage/s, etc are organised. However, it is possible to suggest that the entire monument is of two periods; the higher north-eastern end seems to have been a circular cairn to which the long tail of cairn material, spreading south-westwards, was subsequently added. It is rather more difficult to interpret the spread of cairn material to the north-east, beyond the circuit of the original (?) circular cairn. Only excavation could reveal the true nature of this interesting site.

Visual index 1.   Accessibility 4.

SITE No 37   BENBECULA
BORVE CASTLE   CASTLE   NF773 507

The ruins of Borve Castle lie in the midst of the machair plain about 4km west of Creagorry. Its surviving 10m of height towers over the machair plain, and it is in fact amongst the most massive masonry constructions in the Long Isle. It seems to have been a rectangular tower, measuring 18.3m by 11m, and at least three stories high, as the surviving ruins prove. It is extremely ruinous, its interior so choked with fallen masonry that its original arrangements cannot be discerned. Its history is equally obscure. That it was a residence of the chiefs of the Clan Ranald cannot be doubted, but at what period is quite unknown. Ranald of Benbecula was known in 1625 as Ranald of 'Castleborf', but the date of construction of the site is unknown.

Visual index 4.   Accessibility 1.

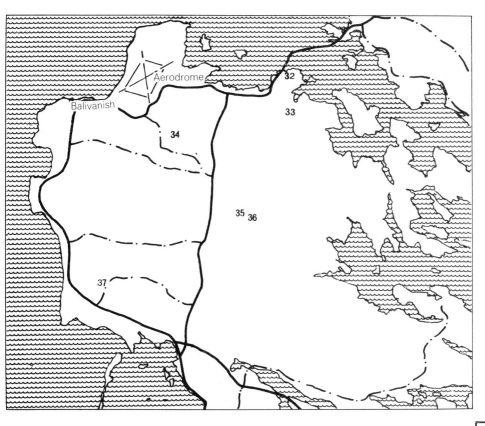

SITE No 38
LOCH A BHARP

PASSAGE GRAVE

SOUTH UIST
NF 777 214

This site lies at the north end of Loch a Bharp and can only be reached by threading one's way across the maze of lochs and burns which feed into Loch Boisdale. The struggle is worth the effort. The cairn survives, 26m in diameter and almost 6m high. Sixteen stones of the kerb survive, two of them fallen. The entrance, on the south side, is marked by a sharp funnel-shaped inturn of the kerb, making a distinct forecourt. Of the entrance passage little can be seen, but the position of the chamber is clearly marked by a circle of corbels, apparently still in their original positions. The chamber is probably oval, and at the exposed level measures approximately 6m by 4m, though it is presumably somewhat larger at its base.

Visual Index 1.   Accessibility 5.

SITE No 39
KILPHEDER

AISLED HOUSE

SOUTH UIST
NF 735 205

This site is marked on the Ordnance Survey 1 in 50,000 map, in the machair west and slightly north of the township of Kilpheder. It occasionally fills in with blown sand and can be hard to find. It consists of a circular house dug into the sand of the machair. It is some 8.8m in diameter and consists of a stone wall, one stone thick, erected to hold back the sand. Within this, eleven stone-built piers are set radially to the circuit of the wall, but not touching it. The gap which results provides the 'aisle' from which this type of wheel_house is named. The piers do not reach the centre of the house. There, a clear circle remains, some 5.5m in diameter, in which the household hearth is set.

Visual index 2 to 5.   Accessibility 2 to 5 (depending on its state).

SITE No 40
CLAIDH HALLAN

16TH CENTURY GRAVE SLAB

SOUTH UIST
NF 734 219

Located in the graveyard at Hallan is one of the handful of sixteenth-century carved grave slabs of the West Highland tradition to find their way to the Western Isles. The slab is covered in ornate foliage.

Visual index 2.   Accessibility 2.

BLoCK

SITE No 41 **SOUTH UIST**
REINAVAL PASSAGE GRAVE NF 755 259

The passage grave of Reinaval lies on
the northern shoulder of the hill of that
name just south of the township of
Mingary. It lies within 200m of the side
road which runs east from the A865 and
south from Mingary. It is conspicuously
sited on the moorland overlooking the
machair and is relatively well preserved.
It is a roughly circular cairn 21m in
diameter and 3.7m high. Some of the
split slabs of the kerb are visible through
the cairn material, especially in the
northern quadrant. Some of these kerb
stones are over 2m high. Part of the
entrance passage can be seen on the
south-east of the cairn. This is 3m long
and a little over 1m wide, being made of
orthostatic slabs. No part of the chamber
is visible and, hopefully, this is preserved
beneath the surviving cairn.

Visual index 1.   Accessibility 1.

SITE No 42   **SOUTH UIST**
HOWMORE CHURCH   CHURCH   NF 758 364

Just beside the village of Howmore, west of the A865, lie a group of interesting
churches and chapels. There are two churches, dedicated to St Mary and St Columba,
and two chapels; a third chapel is known to have stood here, being destroyed shortly
before 1866. The largest church, the most westerly, is represented only by its eastern
gable wall and the foundations of the other walls. It measures 20m by 8m overall and
has two narrow windows in the east wall, set side by side. On either side of the
windows is a small aumbrey or niche. Like the first church, only the eastern wall of
the second survives, in which is a simple window similar to those in the first church.
This church was 3.4m wide, but its length is not now determinable.

The larger of the two chapels measures 5.2m by 3.4m, with walls 0.85m thick. The
entrance, in the east gable, is the trabeate, i.e. it has inwardly inclined door jambs,
just over 1m high and barely 0.4m wide at the top. A window opening, 0.075m wide
and 0.32m high, is set over the door, and there are similar windows in each of the
other walls. The remaining chapel is 3.7m by 2.4m internally with walls 0.80m thick.
Its doorway, also, is trabeate and set in the east gable. The gables are complete and
show that the roof was very steeply pitched. In character these chapels are redolent
of early Celtic sites and the stone-roofed churches of the Irish Early Christian period.
Their close juxtaposition suggests that an Early Christian establishment existed at
Howmore, probably sometime between the late seventh and tenth centuries A.D.

Visual index 1.   Accessibility 1.

This interesting site is on an island in Loch an Eilein south of Drimsdale. The island is about 80m in diameter and bears at its highest point the ruins of a small tower. The latter now stands to a height of 4m and was of at least two stories. The entrance is in the east wall, and beside it is a small window. Two further windows are set in the north wall and one in the west. These are truly small, only 0.18m square, but a smaller ope yet is set in the south wall. This is circular and 0.11m in diameter. The date of the tower is unknown, but one Ronald Alansoun of 'Yland-Bagrim' is mentioned in records of 1505 and 1508. The remainder of the island is occupied by the remains of a number of long houses, presumable blackhouses. Iain Crawford seems to suggest that these were in use contemporaneously with the castle and that Clan Ranald may still have been in residence there up to the end of the seventeenth century.

Visual index 1.   Accessibility 1.

SITE No 44
DUN MOR   DUN FORTIFIED ISLAND

SOUTH UIST
NF 778 415

This site is on an island close to the north shore of Loch an Duin Mhoir just south of the township of West Gerinish. It is approached by a manmade causeway some 1.75m wide and about 42m long. The mid-point of the causeway is often under water. The dun proper is on the south side of the land. It is oval in plan and measures 9.8m north to south and 8.2m east to west, internally. The wall survives to a height of 2.5m on the outside and is 3m thick. The interior is filled with fallen stone, so that little of its architecture can be discerned. Outside the dun and running along the shore of the island is a second wall. This is collapsed and is nowhere higher than 0.60m, though it is now spread over 3m wide, and so may have been much higher at one time. Between the dun and this wall are a number of foundations of what appear to be blackhouses. The impression gained here, as at several of the South Uist duns, is that they were refortified and re-used in the turmoil of the post-medieval period.

Visual index 2.   Accessibility 3.

This dun is sited on a small island in the south-east corner of Loch Uiselan south of the road just west of the township of Ollag. The level of the loch has been much lowered since the construction of the dun, since the causeway to the latter now stands well clear of the water. The dun itself is greatly overgrown and badly knocked about. It appears as a low, stony mound some 18m in diameter and 2.5m high. The loch itself is to a large extent overgrown with reeds. Whilst not particularly interesting from an archaeological point of view, the site has a certain charm.

Visual index 3.   Accessibility 2.

Just left of the road from the A865 to
Eochar, and about 1km west of the
school, a disused bus can be seen in the
garden of a blackhouse. This has been
adorned over every visible surface with
patterns of sea shells. Gazed at for a
short period, this piece of primitive art
moves steadily from eyesore to rurally
charming to high art in the beholder's
estimation. If somewhat naive for
sophisticated tastes, it does have the
merit of being artistically honest, an
epithet not universally applicable to the
world of modern art in Scotland, or
elsewhere. We liked it.

Visual index 1.   Accessibility 1.

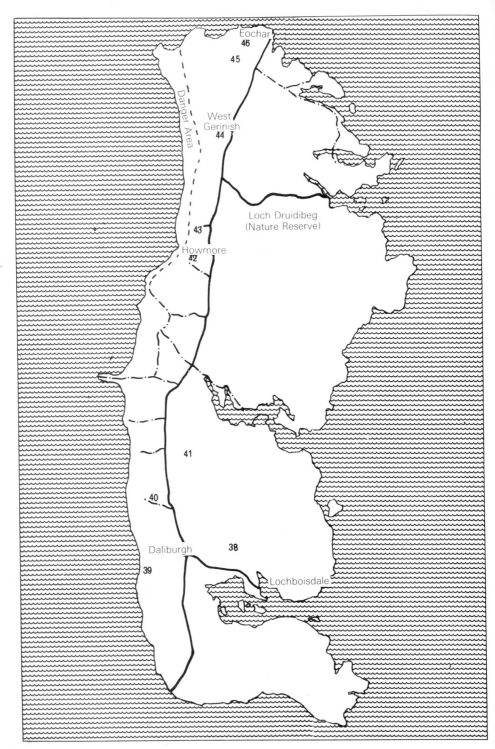

Eochar
46
45

West
Gerinish
44

Danger Area

Loch Druidibeg
(Nature Reserve)

43
Howmore
42

41

40

Daliburgh
38
39

Lochboisdale

SpoT MAP

THE UISTS

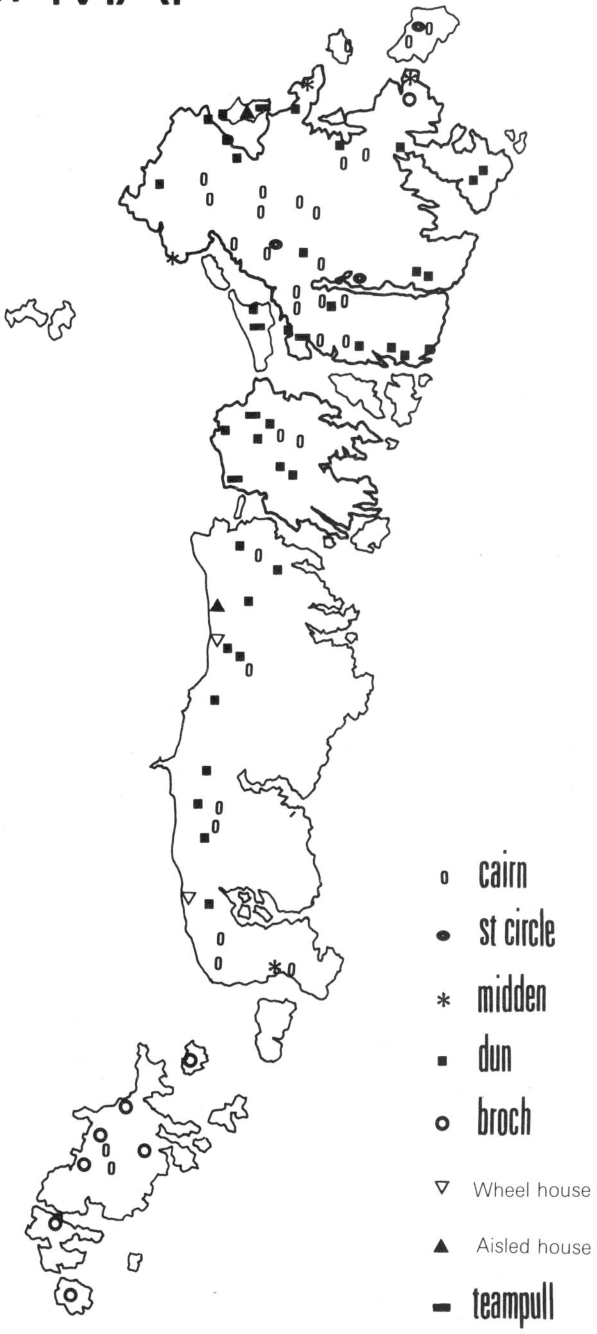

Legend:

- ○ cairn
- ◉ st circle
- ✳ midden
- ■ dun
- ◎ broch
- ▽ Wheel house
- ▲ Aisled house
- — teampull